ALIVE
AND KICKING

Also by Joe Bennett

Just Walking the Dogs (Hazard Press)
Sleeping Dogs and Other Lies (Hazard Press)
Fun Run and Other Oxymorons (Scribner UK)
So Help Me Dog (Hazard Press)
Sit (Hazard Press)
Bedside Lovers (and Other Goats) (Scribner UK)
Doggone (Hazard Press)
Barking (Hazard Press)
A Land of Two Halves (Simon & Schuster UK)
Unmuzzled (Hazard Press)
Dogmatic (Hazard Press)
Mustn't Grumble (Simon & Schuster UK)
Down Boy (Hazard Press)
Eyes Right (and They's Wrong) (HarperCollins)
Where Underpants Come From (Simon & Schuster UK)

ALIVE
AND KICKING

JOE BENNETT

HarperCollins*Publishers*

The columns that make up this collection
first appeared in the *Press*, the *Dominion Post*,
the *Otago Daily Times*, the *Southland Times*,
the *Waikato Daily Times*, *Hawke's Bay Today*,
the *Northern Advocate* and *New Zealand Gardener*.

National Library of New Zealand Cataloguing-in-Publication Data

Bennett, Joe, 1957-
Alive and kicking / Joe Bennett.
ISBN 978-1-86950-672-8
1. New Zealand wit and humor—21st century. 2. New Zealand—
Social life and customs—21st century—Anecdotes. I. Title.
NZ828.202 dc—22

First published 2008
HarperCollins*Publishers (New Zealand) Limited*
P.O. Box 1, Shortland Street, Auckland

ISBN 978 1 86950 672 8

Cover design by Matt Stanton, HarperCollins Design Studio
Typesetting by Janine Brougham

Printed by Griffin Press, Australia
70gsm Classic used by HarperCollins*Publishers*
is a natural, recyclable product made from wood grown in sustainable
forests. The manufacturing processes conform to the environmental
regulations in the country of origin, Finland.

For Baz

CONTENTS

We got it

The door of the council jet swung inwards to leave a hole in the sleek white fuselage. The crowd on the tarmac fell silent.

Into the hole stepped the figure of the Christchurch City Council Administrative Events Contract Negotiation Officer. He paused at the top of the steps. All eyes were on him. Impassively he reached into his jacket and withdrew a wad of paper. Slowly he raised the paper above his head.

'Ratepayers of Christchurch,' he intoned, 'we got it. We got the Turin Motor Show.'

The crowd erupted. The sky went dark with hats flung high. Strangers hugged. There were tears. A young woman ducked under the security cordon, scampered up the steps, flung her arms round the council officer, kissed him square on the lips, placed a garland round his neck and, before dashing away, straightened his comb-over.

Even the security guards were smiling.

The man of the moment stepped up to a microphone. With his finger, he tapped the microphone's bulbous head once, twice. Silence radiated from the core of the crowd to its fringe. The last voice to fall silent was that of a child. 'Daddy,' it said, 'what's a Turin?' Everybody laughed.

'Out of the mouths of babes and suckling ratepayers,' said the council officer, and the crowd grinned. 'But that child has a right to pose the question and I shall answer him. Turin, young man, is an Italian city. It's got the Turin

Shroud and once upon a time it had the Turin Motor Show. But it hasn't got it any more. Do you know who has?'

'We have,' screamed the crowd.

'We have indeed. Just like we've got the Ellerslie Flower Show and the New York Marathon, and just like we oh-so-nearly got the Beijing Olympics.'

Momentarily the crowd's mood slumped as it recalled the last-minute failure of those negotiations.

'But Beijing is behind us,' said the officer, and the eyes of the crowd rose once more to dwell on his face with something close to love, 'and Ellerslie, Turin and New York are in front of us. We at the civic offices are putting your city on the map. Not the South Island map, nor yet the New Zealand map, but the map of the world.'

'Is it true,' asked a shambling journalist, 'that you paid a seven-figure sum for the motor show?'

'Eleven-figure,' said the officer. 'We paid in lire.'

The ratepayers hooted with delight at his deadpan wit.

'And the downstream costs?' asked the journalist.

The crowd hissed. They didn't want to know about downstream costs. But the Council Administrative Events Contract Negotiation Officer silenced the hiss with a single chubby finger.

'That,' he said, addressing the journo with the smug air of one who knows that he has a crowd behind him, 'that, my friend, is the beauty of this business. There are no downstream costs. We didn't buy a single exhibition stand or brochure. Because we didn't buy the Turin Motor Show. We bought,' and here he raised his hands to shoulder level and pecked at the air with the first two fingers of either hand, '"The Turin Motor Show". We bought words. We bought a slug of belief. We bought, my dear old-fashioned friend, a brand.'

'Is it also true,' said the journo, undeterred by the hostility that fizzed around him like static, 'that Turin is planning to hold a motor show as usual?'

'Perhaps they are,' said the officer, 'I don't know. But I do know that it won't be the Turin Motor Show, because that's ours. Just as Ellerslie may hold a garden show, but it won't be the Ellerslie Garden Show. My dear ink-stained friend, has it never crossed your archaic mind that belief is stronger than knowledge and symbols more mighty than truth? Have you never wondered why the Turin Shroud, for example, though long since exposed as a medieval fake, still draws thousands a day to gaze on it? Or why fat people pay good money for All Black shirts, and wear them? And since you're a journalist, have you not noticed that words and their meanings went through the divorce courts years ago? How else could it be that half the Canterbury Crusaders don't come from Canterbury and that none of them crusade? Or that London Bridge stands in the Arizona desert? Or that Mr Peters belongs to a party called New Zealand First?

'Fellow ratepayers, co-habitors of this great city, we live in an age as credulous as any that preceded it, an age of unreason, an age when belief has stolen the garb of thought and struts the streets unchallenged. And we, your representatives at the Christchurch City Council, are proud to have acknowledged and embraced that truth. This document,' and here he waved above his head once more the blessed contract, 'is a piece of our times.'

The crowd, as they say, went ape.

What the head said

Your Grace the Bishop, Board of Governors, staff, parents and pupils, as headmaster of the School of the Globe, it's my duty to report on the academic year that is now ending. And I shall not pussy-foot. I shall say what I think and name names.

So let me begin with a rocket: Africa House, pull your socks up. I've said it before, indeed I have said it every year since 1961, but I shall not stop saying it until those socks come up and a garter fixes each one in a seemly fashion just below the knee as stipulated in the school rules. You could start by selecting a few decent house prefects and finding some way of keeping them honest.

Yes, I am aware of the outbreak of bullying that overran the school in the 17th, 18th and 19th centuries, leading to numerous rival houses installing prefects in Africa House and running the place for their own benefit. It was unpardonable. And I regret that I and the board of governors did not intervene earlier. We were, as our longer-term parents will no doubt recall, preoccupied at the time with the unparalleled expansion of the Science Block.

But all that is now history and it is time for you in Africa House to take responsibility for your own affairs. You generally do pretty well on sports day, except in the swimming pool for some reason, but there is more to life than running and jumping. Your sickbay's a mess, evening prep is a shambles, and your house kitchens are frankly appalling. And if you continue to rely on gifts of tuck and pocket money from squidgy-hearted members of other houses you will continue to flounder.

South America House, as I mentioned in my report last year, seems to be getting somewhere at last, India House even more so, and, if they can, then so can you. All Africa House prefects will report to my study immediately after this assembly.

At the other end of the scale, my congratulations to China House on a simply splendid year. You have motored up the academic league tables. Africa House could profit from studying how you have trebled the length of evening prep and abolished sleeping. You fully deserved getting your name engraved on the Mayor Dafting Cup for Most Improved for the first time since 1306.

There is one matter that concerns me, however. Several incidents have been brought to my attention of junior boys from China House copying work done by scholars from other houses, passing it off as their own and then selling it. This seems to be going on with the connivance of China House prefects and even perhaps the Head of House. The practice is objectionable for several reasons, not the least of which is that most of the pocket money I distribute every Friday now seems to be finding its way to China House, to be then lent out again to boys from Europe House and America House at a rate of interest. The short-term consequences no doubt seem agreeable to all parties, but in the long run it will end in a playground brawl. The practice will stop. If I have to mention it again there will be a few characters dipping their backsides into the Yangtze to cool them. Do I make myself understood?

Talking of playground brawls, I am aware that many of you, and yes, I am addressing myself to America House in particular, take joy in constructing ever more complicated slingshots, pea-shooters and water pistols. Such things are a healthy tradition of boyhood, and I have no plans for mass confiscations. But trade in such items must stop. Trade leads to escalation and someone in the end will get seriously hurt. And surprisingly often, in my experience, it's the trader that suffers. Remember those Exocets, young Britain? I thought so. I don't need to remind you they were made by someone sleeping in the same dorm as you.

Now to a matter that concerns every single member of the school: the big clean-up of campus. It is long overdue, and I accept full responsibility for letting things slide. Thirty or 40 years ago, and blinded by the new technology curriculum, we entertained vague notions of shifting to a new campus entirely. We now acknowledge that we were deluded. This will not happen. Scrubbing brushes are being delivered to every house and I shall expect a cleaning roster to be drawn up by prefects. And this applies to all of you, America House included. The future of the school depends on it.

One other thing, chapel has been abolished. I know it will be an unpopular move especially in Middle East House and America House, but the board has resolved, with only the bishop dissenting, that it was a misguided educational experiment that's never done any good. All chapels will be dismantled by school staff over the summer break. I wish you all a happy holiday.

Here are some questions

Forget Sudoku. Ditch the crossword. Today's little brainteaser is to find the odd one out in the following list of questions. Answers on a postcard, please, to the editor, who, the poor darling, is just desperate for correspondence.

Do you lust after my armpits? Does anyone lust after my armpits? Were the raids on the Ureweras racist? Do people who use the word racist pay any attention to its actual meaning? Does the word still serve any useful function? How are you going so far?

(Sorry, that last question does not belong among the questions. It was just an instinctive expression of cordiality, of sympathy, in this hostile and puzzling world. It should be inside these insulating brackets.)

If the people arrested in the Ureweras had napalm, were the authorities justified in going after them under the Suppression of Terrorism Act? Is the Suppression of Terrorism Act a good piece of legislation? Should it be allowed to persist on the Statute Book? Will it be erased from the Statute Book? Are laws commonly erased from the Statute Book when they are seen to be outdated or dangerous or just wrong? Will the time ever come when we consider we have enough laws and all that is required thenceforth from our lawmakers is that they sit back, twiddle their thumbs, trade the odd insult, nip out into the corridor for a stoush when they're feeling stroppy and draw nice salaries that no one will resent so long as the law-makers do nothing except dust the Statute Book occasionally? Should Statute Book have capital letters? Getting warmer?

(That last does not belong among the questions either. It was designed merely to urge you to persist because I realise that this interrogative barrage is imposing an unfair strain on your cerebellum when it's already got plenty to chew on, from Britney Spears to global warming. But I've started so I shall finish.)

If you've started something does it therefore follow that you should finish it? Is Britney Spears worth thinking about? Is Britney Spears related to global warming? Will you do your bit to diminish global warming without being forced to do it? Should you be forced to do your bit? Are we, the human race, good at addressing intangibles even if they are likely to become tangibles in the foreseeable future? Is the foreseeable future a phrase that makes sense? Does even the word sense make sense in a chaotic world driven by blind forces?

(Look, I'm sorry to interrupt again, but I would like to apologise for getting on to the big stuff so rapidly. I had intended to keep it all nice and concrete, all Britney Spears and napalm, if you like — and I, for one, like them both equally — but it is a remarkable feature of posing questions that they inevitably spiral backwards and expand as they go and lead you unstoppably to the great imponderables that the more reflective members of the human race have always insisted on pondering to no effect. I'll try and keep things simple but I make no promises.)

Will I succeed in keeping things simple? Are most

promises kept? Are the great imponderables worth pondering? Did the All Blacks win the World Cup? (Ah, that's better. That's more like it.)

When I use the phrase 'That's more like it', have I any idea what the it refers to? When the All Blacks lost the World Cup did it matter? As a result of the loss will we cease to consider the All Blacks as something akin to the disciples in shorts, people so close to and intimate with the godhead that they are themselves quasi-divine? Will we at the same time cease to place on them a burden of national identity that is obviously too heavy even for their gym-inflated shoulders? Is national identity a good thing? Is it anything other than a consoling fiction? Is there anything that the 4,000,000 people on these islands have in common apart from being on these islands? Has a sense of national identity ever achieved anything other than triumphalism and conflict? Have we as a race ever progressed beyond tribalism? Will we progress beyond tribalism before the planet dries up, burns off or implodes? Do I care? Am I sad? Have you had enough of these questions?

(Oh good, I am pleased. And that answer is a big fat clue for those of you who may still be struggling.)

Is it conceivable that anyone who is still struggling would still be reading? And will I put such people, if indeed there are any, out of their misery by telling them the answer? And am I about to take the dog out for the simple pleasure of doing so, mine and his?

Fanks

'We're stoked to have got him,' said the vice-chancellor of Wellington University, 'and our Department of Androgyny is especially thrilled. Half the universities in the world were after him. You saw what happened when he came here recently to play football: our target market just fell about in adoration. He's a natural communicator. The university council was unanimous in its decision to offer him the chancellorship in perpetuity. He accepted by satellite link from his private jet, and he did so with a humble simplicity which we think bodes rather well. "Fanks," he said.

'Naturally we will continue to offer traditional academic disciplines such as tourism, aromatherapy and real estate, but following his appointment we have established exciting new subject areas and they are proving popular. Our degree courses in brand awareness and male cosmetics are already oversubscribed and we're having to build a new block to house tattoo studies.'

'Don't be absurd,' said the resident conductor of the Chicago Symphony Orchestra. 'Of course he won't be required to play. He won't even be required to hold an instrument. But having him sit in the first violin's chair is going to bring a whole new audience to classical music. I gather that his wife is a singer, but it's him we want. He is music in football shorts. He's a visual concerto. That naughty grin of his is a score just seeking notation. And boy, has he pulled in the sponsors! Gillette just couldn't wait to get in behind our Beethoven series. Music to Shave To, it's called, and I do urge you to attend. At the climax of the Eroica, he's going to take his shirt off.'

'The Security Council didn't hesitate for a moment,' said Ding Dong, chairman of the UN. 'Professional sport, you see, is the most effective narcotic in the peacemaker's armoury. By mimicking warfare, it acts as a channel for testosterone overflow. And it appeals most strongly to our problem demographic, males in their 20s. To put things as simply as I can, if they're watching a football match they're not blowing things up. So appointing him as UN Special Envoy to the Middle East seemed as obvious to us as charging dinner to an expense account. And we were delighted by his immediate acceptance. "Fanks," he said.'

'Their former royal highnesses,' said a Palace spokesman, 'accepted their demotion with the good grace that has been the hallmark of their tenure. They understood that is always better to precipitate change than to wait until change is forced upon one. Of course the new regime has meant a significant adjustment to palace protocol, but one has actually found it quite refreshing. The newly appointed Royal Corps of Hairdressers, in particular, have brought a degree of hilarity to the inner sanctum that has been enjoyed by all. Golly, how they squeal! Admittedly it is tiresome having the Mall lined day and night with fainting pre pubescent girls but the Household Cavalry has quickly acquired some expertise in resuscitation techniques.'

'There was no power struggle, as you put it,' said

a Vatican spokesman. 'Pope Benedict volunteered to stand down. And the effect is already apparent. Angelic, telegenic and incontrovertibly heterosexual, our new Holy Father ticks all the boxes. We've never had so many applications from would-be nuns. But it's in South America, our traditional economic base, where he's working his most powerful miracles. They worship football down there, and now that they've got a pope with an educated right boot, they're cramming the pews and, more importantly, the coffers.'

'To be frank, I neither understand nor appreciate the sceptical tone of your question, and I would advise you to be a little more polite,' said a life form representing the Extra Terrestrial Colonisation Society. 'But to answer your question with more respect than it perhaps deserves, when we studied Earth and its temporarily dominant species, this specimen simply stood out. It was clear that he spoke to his fellow creatures in a pre-verbal fashion. The light of reason has never been more than a glimmer in your primitive kind. You've still got both feet in the swamp. So when confronted by an archetype of adolescent beauty who is also an athletic warrior king, you go gaga. Furthermore this particular specimen and his mate embody the doomed consumptive habits of your prevailing cultural system, so we had no hesitation in selecting him. When, quite soon, we decide to beam down and take control we shall immediately install him as the first Emperor of Planet Earth. He'll be no more than a puppet, of course, and he will not be required to make speeches, but he'll serve our needs nicely.'

Citing a hectic academic, artistic, diplomatic, royal, religious and intergalactic schedule, David Beckham declined to comment on any of his new appointments, but he expressed his gratitude for the good wishes. 'Fanks,' he said.

Among fish

My shoulders are crimson from staring at fish. It's a small price to pay for wonder.

You've seen tropical aquariums populated by tiny shoals of electric fish of improbable patterns and shapes. Most of those fish come from the Philippines and I have just seen them, here where they live, among coral in the Philippine Sea.

With three Filipinos I rented a boat for what they call island hopping. We would go over there first for snorkelling, then there to explore caves, then there to body surf, and there for lunch. Well, we went over there for snorkelling then just stayed there because of me.

I last snorkelled as a child. The mask misted over, I forgot not to breathe through my nose, I swallowed pints and I've never done it since. Snorkelling was aquatic panic.

We moored at a buoy. Half a dozen other boats lilted nearby and the water was as clear as water should be. The boatman tossed pellets of bread overboard and instantly the surface seethed with brilliantly coloured fish, like a jeweller's window in an earthquake.

I was over the side before you could say mask, snorkel and flotation vest. I held a fistful of bread. Crumbs drifted from my fingers and the fish flocked, nibbling my knuckles, knocking my mask, darting from my armpit. Because of the fish I forgot to think about snorkelling. Because I forgot to think about snorkelling I snorkelled fine.

Slowing my breathing to perhaps four breaths a minute, I just lay there inert, enveloped by fish. The only sound was the whaaah of my breath through the tube.

The fish proved fairweather friends. When the bread was gone so were they. The water cleared to reveal a sea-sized aquarium, and I was in it.

Like every fisherman I have stared into countless stretches of water. I have watched carp roll, trout feed and pike lurk among bulrushes. I have held my breath watching all of these things. But never have I felt as I felt now in the blood-warm Philippine Sea, that I was among the fish, that I was truly in the water, part of its world.

I am not much given to wonder. The officially wondrous sights — the views, the cathedrals, the monumental things — don't spin my wheels much. 'Ah ha,' I say, 'that's pretty enough', but I'm holding a sagging stalk of disappointment. Here, however, I was face down in a new world.

The point was not its beauty but its otherness. This element was not my element. I remained umbilically linked by the snorkel to the world I inhabited, but my senses were all below, my ears, my eyes, my skin, in a new inverted world where the fish swam through a different landscape. For the half-century that I have lived in the air above, billions of fish have been down here doing this, being different, being other.

A five-fingered starfish lay draped over a rock. It was bright blue. And nosing, pecking, grazing this seascape was a history of haphazard evolution. Here were fish with snouts as long as their bodies, fish striped like zebras or hooped like rugby jerseys, and a fish a yard long, an inch thick and the colour of frost. Here were yellow rectangular fish like beer mats on their sides, angel fish, fish the colour of a welding flame, and, writhing from a den in the coral, a fat and predatory eel in skin corrugated like a ducting pipe. And I was among these fish.

Steering with little kicks, I followed a nosing brown puffer fish for perhaps half an Earth hour. Its body was a bloated shoebox and its gill fins fluttered like fans.

I know I haven't conveyed my sense of wonder. I didn't expect to. There are no words in the sea.

A couple of times I heard my friends calling from the boat. Their voices came from somewhere so remote that they were easy to ignore. When eventually they launched a canoe to fetch me I had drifted perhaps half a mile from the boat. My shoulders, thighs and calves had remained exposed to the different world of sun and air and were burnt to the point of pain. I didn't care. I still don't. Stigmata.

Jumper

The movie that took most money at the box offices of the world last week was *Jumper*. I went to see it. You don't need to know why.

What's *Jumper* about? Well, it's about one and a half hours. But I spent more than one and a half hours pondering what it meant. I decided it meant that, perhaps three years ago in Los Angeles, a man with an idea must have met a man with money and had the following conversation.

Idea Man: Hello, I've got an idea for a movie. It's called *Jumper*.

Money Man: Is it about a frog?

Idea Man: No.

Money Man: Is it about knitting?

Idea Man: No. It's about a shy schoolboy who fancies a pretty girl in his class.

Money Man: A promising cliché.

Idea Man: Thank you. Unfortunately, the shy school-boy falls through some ice and looks sure to drown, but then. . .

Money Man: I'm all ears.

Idea Man: Oh, I wouldn't say that. They may stick out a bit, but I think they make you look distinguished. They reflect the bulge in your wallet.

Money Man: Thank you. But do please tell me what happens to the shy schoolboy who's drowning.

Idea Man: He goes to the library.

Money Man: I see.

Idea Man: No, you don't. One moment he is drowning in an icy river, the next he is gasping on the floor of the library. He jumps, you see.

Money Man: He jumps from the river to the library?

Idea Man: Yes. Instantaneously. And he soon discovers that he can jump at will. He just has to think of a place, anywhere in the world, and he suddenly jumps there, accompanied only by a whooshing noise, and the occasional chunk of rubble that never seems to hit him.

Money Man: How does he do this jumping?

Idea Man: That's not explained. But it's a useful skill. When Jumper wants some money he thinks of a bank vault and suddenly he's in the bank vault. He steals a lot of money then thinks of home and suddenly he's home again. So now he has unlimited cash to go with his unlimited freedom. All he lacks is. . .

Money Man: the girl.

Idea Man: You should write movies yourself. He fetches the girl and takes her to Yerp.

Money Man: Yerp?

Idea Man: Yes, Yerp. But only the pretty bits like Rome. Everything seems fine.

Money Man: But?

Idea Man: But in Rome he discovers that he isn't the only Jumper in the world. And he further discovers that there are people whose mission in life is to kill Jumpers. They're called Paladins.

Money Man: Weren't Paladins medieval knights?

Idea Man: Yes.

Money Man: Why do Paladins want to kill Jumpers?

Idea Man: That is not explained.

Money Man: How do people become Paladins?

Idea Man: That is not explained.

Money Man: Do Paladins look like medieval knights?

Idea Man: No, they look like Americans. The principal Paladin is a black man with white hair. He has high-tech devices for hunting Jumpers with, but when he catches one he stabs it to death with a low-tech hunting knife.

Money Man: Why does he do that?

Idea Man: It makes a more gruesome movie.

Money Man: Does he stab our Jumper?

Idea Man: No, because our Jumper looks like a young Mel Gibson. At the end of the movie Jumper goes to find his mom, who — did I mention this? — ran away when Jumper was five, leaving him in the unsatisfactory care of a no-good father. It turns out that Mom ran away because she was a Paladin and so she would have been obliged to kill her Jumper son.

Money Man: How did she become a Paladin and how did a Paladin give birth to a Jumper?

Idea Man: These things are not explained.

Money Man: Is that it?

Idea Man: Yes. The story's got romance, special effects, fantasy, drama and medieval mysticism along the lines of *The Da Vinci Code* and similar top-notch literature. Furthermore, since the Jumper, his Paladin mom and the black Paladin with white hair are all still alive at the end of the movie, we've got scope for *Jumper the Sequel*, *Jumper Returns* and *Jumper the Sequel the Sequel*. What do you think?

Money Man: I think it's without merit of any kind. I

think it's the most tedious derivative tosh I have heard in my life. I think you're presuming that the cinema-going audience is effectively brain-dead. I think every bit of it screams stupidity.

Idea Man: Thank you.

Money Man: And I think that in three years' time it will be the most popular movie in the world. Here's a blank cheque.

Bin there, done that

'I'll get Osama bin Laden,' said John McCain, candidate for the Republican presidential nomination, 'if I have to go to the gates of hell.' The crowd roared with delight.

Now, I'm as moved by biblical imagery and wild promises as the next man, but I couldn't help feeling a little sorry for McCain. He may get the Republican nomination but I'm afraid he won't get Osama. You see, I've already got him. I probably should have mentioned it before, but a few months ago I got so fed up with the whole bin Laden carry-on that I simply went and killed the devil incarnate myself. It was fairly straightforward.

I packed the essentials — a Bible, the crucifix fashioned for me by blind Fabricius of Smyrna, my trusty stilettos, a couple of T-bone steaks, some garlic and a sachet of strychnine — flew Air New Zealand to Karachi, then headed into the hills on a local bus with seats made from what felt like yak bone. But you have to suffer to assassinate.

I wasn't sure whether the settlement I reached was in Pakistan or Afghanistan but then neither were the locals. It doesn't seem to matter much up there, what with them not getting newspapers or following the cricket. To break the ice I organised a pick-up game of rugby using a goat bladder. They loved it. When they were all relaxing afterwards I casually asked after Osama. They turned and stared at one of the locks. He had a bit of a limp but he was tall and he had given a decent shove in the scrum.

'Osama?' I exclaimed, 'the devil incarnate at the gates of hell?'

'The same,' he said and he gave a little bow, then invited me to his place. It was a basic yurt, but in one corner was the hub of his sophisticated communications system so often mentioned in the press.

'Nice cellphone,' I said.

'You've got to be joking,' said Osama, 'the coverage up here is dreadful.'

He took down a video and slid it into his machine. It was dated four years from now and starred himself sitting cross-legged with a Kalashnikov and spouting the usual stuff about death to the infidel. He sat down cross-legged in front of it.

'Fancy a bite to eat?' I said, pulling a steak from my bag. The way his eyes lit up was a treat to watch. I doubt he'd had a good feed in months.

'Coming right up,' I said. I seared the steaks to retain the juices, before frying them with the garlic. Then I smeared one of them liberally with strychnine and handed it to old Osama. He ate without taking his eyes from the screen.

I waited for the familiar symptoms, the muscle spasms, the convulsions, the rictus. Nothing.

'How's the steak?'

'Fine,' he said, 'I appreciate the garlic. But at the risk of seeming rude I think you've been a little heavy-handed with the strychnine.' The moment he spoke he reared to his feet. And he had 10 horns and seven heads with seven diadems upon his head and on his forehead was tattooed the number of the beast and it was 666.

'Steady on,' I said, but there was no placating him. His tail swept down a third of the stars of heaven, exactly as predicted in the Book of Revelation, Chapter 12, verse 4, and cast them to the Earth.

I reached instinctively for my stiletto with its blade of Toledo steel. Many a fatal rib thrust has that little beauty delivered. But it was flung from my hand by some superhuman force before I'd even managed to get it off my foot.

'Who is like the beast and who can fight against it?' roared Osama, quoting with impressive accuracy for a Muslim from Revelation 13, verse 4. I felt theologically out of my depth. My hand went to my heart and met the old iron cross that Fabricius of Smyrna fashioned for me so many moons ago. I thrust it out in front of me, along with the Bible and a clove of garlic left over from the cooking. The beast, Osama, the dragon, whatever it was, recoiled and seemed momentarily blinded. Sensing that it was now or never, I grabbed my untouched steak and plunged it through his heart, driving it home with the heel of my other stiletto. He squirmed, screamed in a manner that I cannot reproduce in words, passed through a thousand shapes and patterns, each more ghastly than the last, then shuddered and shrivelled and fell dead on the floor of the yurt, shrunk once more to mortal dimensions. I tossed him straightway into the lake of fire and brimstone where, according to Revelation 20, verse 10, he will be tormented day and night for ever and ever, then I collected my stuff, turned off the video, toddled down the hill and caught the bus back to Karachi.

Sorry, John. I should have said.

_Ed_

You wouldn't believe how many people have stopped me in the street following last week's account of my assassination of Osama bin Laden, and said it was the most thrilling adventure story they'd read since the Three Little Pigs. Did I have any more?

Does the Earth go round the sun? I've got more adventure stories than the Pope has dresses. But sadly the laws of libel, slander, malfeasance nunc and fealty pro tem (in excelsis deo) forbid all the juicier ones from seeing the light.

For example, I have no doubt that the world would be agog to hear how I posed as an Arab businessman and squirrelled my way into intimacy with Princess Di. Oh, the vitriol fired at me by the royal hangers-on, who are just fine with dusky skin tones so long as they're arrayed in native costume and doing a bit of jigging with spears to welcome the white goddess from the silver sky-bird, but who find duskiness a bit less endearing when it's bedding one of their own. Di's mum, a real old-style toff with more hyphens than name, was particularly venomous. She called me a wop bed-hopper, along with a couple of epithets that I can't divulge for legal reasons but that would melt the frames on your horn-rimmed.

Though actually the toughest part was the fake tan. It goes without saying that it had to be an all-over tan. That Di was one very thorough People's Princess. You might have thought that the doe-eyed mother of two would be preoccupied at the time with sheltering her little ones from the cruelties of the media as she went through the most public divorce in history, but not a bit of it. The Queen of Hearts was a good-time gal.

On my yacht in the Caribbean one afternoon I thought the game was up when she discovered a pale patch between my toes, but I managed to weasel round it with a fabrication I'm still proud of. You know how Othello, another dark chap, zonked Desdemona with stories of the Anthropophagi whose heads did grow beneath their shoulders, well I spun Di a beauty about my battle with a giant cobra in the Punjab that ended with me being bitten on the toe, hence the scar. I went on to explain how I'd sucked the wound clean myself, a contortion rendered possible by seven years and seven days of study under a Nepalese yogi. Di swallowed it whole. But with the lunatic court case going on in London at the moment I'm afraid further details will have to remain under wraps.

Talking of Nepal reminds me of that time in the early 1950s when I was sauntering down from the summit of Everest, lugging a brace of Sherpas who'd succumbed to oxygen deficiency. Well, who should I meet but Ed, as he then was, on the way up with Tenzing. We exchanged chat, as you do. I told them it was a tad nippy at the top but the views were worth it, and we parted the best of friends.

But when Ed turned to belay up the overhang, he accidentally caught me with the handle of his ice-axe. It wasn't much of a blow but what with a Sherpa over each shoulder I was a little top-heavy and I tumbled into a crevasse. There was nothing that Ed and Tenzing could do. As I fell I shouted to them to keep going and not to worry, I'd be fine.

The story of my three-month crawl down the glacier, dragging myself and the Sherpas along by the only bone left unbroken in my body, a small one in the ear, will have to wait for the autobiography. But when we eventually returned to civilisation I made a point of getting in touch with Sir Ed, as he was by then, to show there were no hard feelings. We had a cracking evening. How we roared over that line he gave the press: 'We knocked the bastard off.' It had been his way of indirectly paying tribute to yours truly. Though he confessed that he rather wished I'd got down safely before him and received the world's acclaim. He loved climbing but loathed the fuss.

We met often after that. In recent years he was increasingly distressed by the palaver that his death was going to cause. 'Every God-freak, politician, columnist and television toady will want to get in on it,' he said. 'They'll go on and on, and it will all be the most terrible mythologising tosh.'

'At least you won't have to listen to it,' I said.

'Perhaps,' he said, 'but it's you lot I feel sorry for.' Which was rather typical of the old boy. He was one of the good guys.

Champs

You can hardly fail to have noticed by now that *New Zealand Garden*, or whatever it's called — though I write for the thing, I never read it myself for obvious reasons — has been judged the best magazine in the country. It is officially better than *Bridal Monthly*, *Rugby Week*, and *Stamp Collecting Quarterly* and here's how it happened.

A couple of months ago I got a phone call from an editor who didn't at the time know that she was about to be judged best editor in the universe, and editor, not uncoincidentally, of the universe's best mag.

'Fancy a beano, Joe?' she said. 'In Auckland.'

'Golly,' I said. 'Little old me in Sin City? Where the traffic is dizzying, the cocktails purple and the sidewalks paved with television newsreaders?'

'You're a finalist,' she said. 'In the magazine columnist awards.'

'Golly,' I said again, which I know impressed her. 'For writing about dead cats in a gardening mag?'

'Yes,' she said, because that's how editors speak: forthright; terse; emphatic. 'Are you up for it?'

'Of course not,' I said. 'What is there for me in Auckland?'

'Unlimited booze and it's all on us,' said the editor.

'See you there,' I said. 'Thank you very much indeed, Your Excellency', because that's the manly and independent way I talk to editors.

At university, whenever I pulled on a rented dinner jacket and wrapped a bow-tie about my peach-skin neck,

I knew for certain that three hours later I would be drunk as a skunk and snoring face down in a flower bed, having prepared for sleep by vomiting extensively and losing a shoe.

These days, aged 50, I now own my dinner jacket and I wrap the bow-tie about a grizzled neck. Otherwise nothing has changed. I have never yet dressed formally and gone to bed sober.

If you missed the television coverage, let me tell you that the event sparkled. At a guess there were 1000 of the great and good assembled in Auckland's plushest hotel, 1000 famous magazine faces of which I recognised approximately none. But it was easy to pick out the editors, from their stately bearing, stunning attire, and the way they drank straight from the bottle.

The evening was hosted by a woman who sang opera for no reason and then dished out the awards, starting with the insignificant and building towards the supremely significant.

'Our first award of the evening,' she said, 'is for columnist of the year. And it goes to *Little Treasures* columnist . . .' but the name was lost amid the acclamation. You can imagine my relief. Not only would I not be waking up beside an ugly trophy and a cheque, but I also had the joy of knowing that the award had gone to someone who wrote about babies. I expressed my relief by going to the bar. Service must have been slow, because when I returned to my table I found that I'd missed rather a lot of awards. This mag had already been crowned the year's best special interest mag — which always sounds to me like code for sadomasochism — and my editor had become editor of the year. All that remained was the big one, what Spanish lottery ticket sellers call El Gordo.

'And magazine of the year 2007,'. . . pause while the St John chaps defibrillated a couple of circulation managers, 'goes to . . . ' drumroll . . . unspeakable tension . . . more drumroll . . .

Well, when the name of this mag, whatever it is, was read out, you can imagine the scene. An Etna of champers drenched the chandeliers, glasses flew, editors swooned, shouts of 'Attaboy' and 'Dig that border' rang out, while the *Bridal Monthly* table slunk off en masse unnoticed to mutter and sulk.

Only they didn't, of course. Readers of *Bridal Monthly* aren't going to say, 'Oh, I see that gardening thing's the best mag in the country, I'd better buy it. Oh and while I'm at it I'll cancel my subscription to *BM*.' (Actually I wonder whether anyone does have a subscription to *Bridal Monthly*. If so, I think men should be told.)

Once the festivities were over and my sainted editor had made a speech outlining her plans for world peace, all that was left for me to do was Auckland. Armed only with hope, I went in search of Sin City and found it. I had a ball. And I can cheerfully report that most of the stains on the dinner jacket have come out quite nicely, the bow-tie won't cost much to replace, whoever finds my shoe is welcome to it, and Albert Park does a very comfortable line in flower beds. When I woke amid peonies that may, on reflection, have been delphiniums, for the first time in my life I felt like a true gardening columnist.

Cardiosanguiniensis cunctatus optatus

It's a disease of Western affluence. It may be the most contagious virus ever known. It sweeps suddenly through whole populations. It severely debilitates the rational mind. And yet it has undergone little study. The few medical researchers in the field know it as Cardiosanguiniensis cunctatus optatus, or selective, delayed-onset, bleeding of the heart.

The most remarkable characteristic of this disease is that its apparent cause is not its true cause. Take, for example, the epidemic that has swept through the West in the last few weeks. The apparent cause is Chinese repression of Tibet. But the true cause is harder to define.

Part of it is simply exposure to the virus through the media. The media themselves are immune but they suffer from a mimic virus that exhibits all the external symptoms of bleeding from the heart — grave looks on newsreaders' faces, earnest editorial tones — but involves no actual bleeding. Nor, indeed, does it involve a heart, but rather a stoutly beating commercial nerve.

How exposure to the mimic virus spreads the virus proper through the general population is not yet understood. Current research suggests that the virus attaches itself to the bandwagonicus gene, the gene that dictates the human instinct for following the herd. At the same time the virus generates a warm sense of virtue in the host for championing an underdog.

That pleasant feeling may explain why the immune system does not attack the virus. The immune system simply does not recognise it as hostile to brain function. But brain function is severely affected. The virus causes the brain to simplify the world into good and bad. The host then sides with the good.

If we return for a moment to the disease's full clinical name, note the term cunctatus, meaning delayed-onset. The West has had plenty of time to feel sorry for Tibet. Even if we ignore the history of Chinese involvement with Tibet, which goes back 1000 years or more (glossing over as we go the British military expedition to Tibet in 1904 when the brave Brits mowed down 1000 or more peaceable Tibetans with the newly invented machine gun), and if we concern ourselves only with current Chinese occupation (which began, I might add, with what was effectively an agreement between the Tibetans and the Chinese and which included a period when the Tibetans were covertly backed against the Chinese by the CIA), we have still had over 50 years to feel sorry for Tibet. For most of us that's our entire lives.

I am not arguing that the Tibetans do not have a case. Nor am I arguing that the Chinese rulers are nice. I am merely pointing out that Tibet has suddenly become everyone's cause du jour, after 18,000 similar jours when it was very few people's cause. That's how the virus works. It is sudden, arbitrary and selective.

It pays no attention, for example, to Xinjiang, another supposedly autonomous region of China in which the indigenous Uighurs regularly rise against their Chinese rulers and are brutally put down. This may be because the

West finds it harder to bleed from the heart for Muslims than for Buddhists, just as the West is slow to save an endangered species of spider, but rushes to the cause of endangered furry mammals.

The virus is also fickle. Within a month or two Tibet will drop from the view of the herd and hearts will start bleeding instead for the Inuit Indians, perhaps, or the three-toed sloth. Neither the Inuits nor the sloths will profit.

The bleeding of the heart is harmless. But other symptoms of the virus are less appealing. The ugliest of these is hypocrisy. Those suffering from the virus often require others to act as consciences on their behalf. This is illustrated in the present epidemic by sufferers calling for New Zealand athletes to boycott the Olympics.

One has to feel sorry for the athletes. There they are, approaching the pinnacle of their brief careers in strange activities, when suddenly they are asked to give it all up by people who plan to give up nothing themselves. Moreover those same people have spent the last 20 years or more cheerfully trotting down to Farmers and Bunnings to snap up cheap Chinese underwear and cheap Chinese power tools, and are even now probably eyeing up a cheap Chinese wide-screen high-definition plasma television on which to watch the Olympics, without ever giving a thought to the way they have been supporting a regime that the virus is now causing them to denounce from the pulpit of moral superiority and general ignorance. It's not a pretty sight. More research into this terrible contagion is urgently needed.

How kind are you?

On a scale of 1 to 4, how kind are you? Oh really? You're sure? Well, congratulations. But if you're not sure, read on.

I'm asking about kindness because my mother rang to thank me for sending her two postcards.

'Two?' I said.

'Two,' she said.

'But I only sent one,' I said, and then I remembered and I smiled and I said, 'Good, so there's hope.'

There's hope that the world may yet be right way up. Though Americans may fail to see through Hillary Clinton, though Hagley Park may be overrun by boy racers with giant exhausts and tiny gearsticks, though Tony Blair may become Earth's special envoy to the galaxy, though Kiwis may buy Steinlager because an American actor tells them to, though the People's Republic of Cuba may replace, in the name of the people, President Castro with President Castro, though *Dancing with the Stars* may find its way onto the front page of what was once a newspaper, yet there is hope.

A few weeks ago, you see, in Auckland, I bought a postcard, wrote a few words on it, stamped it and addressed it to my mother. She's 84. At 84 you don't want things, but you do want to be loved. From bassinet to crematorium we all want to be loved. And postcards can be tokens of love.

I found a postbox, despite the fact that they seem to become sparser every year, reached into my pocket and pulled out some shrivelled bits of dog food. But no postcard. It must have fallen into an Auckland gutter. So I bought another card and posted that, and felt that I had done a little kindness.

But the lost card, lying on the ground, stamped and ready to go, must have caught someone's eye, and he or she did a greater kindness. He or she must have gone to the trouble of finding a postbox and popping it in.

I forget who said the greatest pleasure in life was to be caught doing good by stealth. Well, whoever posted my card will never know that pleasure. He went out of his way to add something to the sum of human happiness but he sought no acknowledgment. The question to ask is why?

My puppy would never do such a thing. Though the puppy appears to dote on me it is only because I control his access to the good things in life: food, games and furniture to chew. His motto is Darwinian: 'What's in it for me?' That also happens to be the motto of commerce. But it can never be the motto of society as a whole. Because it is kindness that makes human civilisation possible. Kindness means recognising the needs of others. Kindness underlies courtesy, and the rule of law. Kindness in one form or another must happen constantly and unnoticed as we go about our lives, because without it there can be no trust. And without trust, civilisation crumbles. Without it, we cannot live together. Without it, this world is dog eat dog. Without it we would all wear guns.

So, if you want to know how kind a citizen you are, complete the following rigorously scientific multi-choice questionnaire.

If you had found my postcard would you have posted it?

    a.   You've got to be joking.

    b.   Yes, if it was lying close to a postbox.

    c.   Yes.

    d.   Yes, even if I'd had to walk 50 miles to the postbox in bare feet over cobra-infested broken glass.

Before posting it, would you have read it?

    a.   I can't read.

    b.   Of course.

    c.   Yes, but guiltily.

    d.   No.

If you found $20 in the street would you

    a.   whoop with delight and go straight to the pub, pausing en route only to look for a stamped, addressed postcard to use as a beer mat?

    b.   kneel, pretend to tie up your shoelace and slip the note into your pocket?

    c.   sit down nearby, wait five minutes to see if anyone came looking for it, then pocket it, take it home and wait for the guilt to die down?

    d.   pick it up, wave it above your head in search of the owner, then give it to charity?

If you answered 'a' to all the above you are a dog. There is nothing wrong with being a dog. Dogs are honest. If you answered 'd' you are either a saint or dishonest. But if you answered 'b' or 'c' you lie somewhere on the muddied scale of humanity, between absolute kindness at one end and absolute selfishness at the other, along with all the rest of us. And if you recently picked up a postcard in Auckland and posted it, please let me know. I want to kiss you.

Alarmed

I've just met a shed for our times. It stands in a little bay that I've avoided since I met a lunatic there. He threatened me and tried to kidnap my dog. He had a beard of course, and eyes like lollipops. Whenever I thought of going back there I thought of those eyes and went elsewhere, which is a pity because the bay is a good place for dogs. There are rabbits. I once lost two dogs there for an hour. When I found them only their rear ends were visible above ground, their tails whipping. The front ends were deep down a rabbit burrow, digging. Earth and blood lust had rendered them deaf.

Anyway, I finally returned to the bay the other midnight. I scanned the place from above for gleaming lollipops but saw only a shed that hadn't been there before. Call me reckless but I decided to risk the possibility that Mr Lollipop was inside the shed.

He wasn't. The shed was locked. It was also stencilled with a phrase in capital letters. 'THIS SHED IS ALARMED', it said.

'You and everyone else, shed,' I said.

How alarmed are you on a scale of 1 to 100, where 1 means you have the placidity of a doughnut, and 100 means you feel like an infant koala in a cage of cougars? If your score is anything under 80 you're a failure. As a citizen of the prosperous West, as an exemplum of the chosen few who have never, in the history of the species, had it so good, it is your duty to be alarmed. If you're not alarmed, if you're not quivering with dreads both specified and unspecified, you just haven't been paying enough attention. You haven't been dutiful. Open your eyes.

How Clean is Your House? is the title of a television programme. 'Filthy,' I say, 'but thank you so much for asking', and change channel, so I haven't watched the programme. I don't need to. It's obvious what happens. Someone moderately telegenic, a woman, I suspect, but with her hair severely tied back and a pair of glasses she may or may not need, and a white lab coat because a white lab coat means science, gets down on her pretty knees, the lab coat tautening provocatively over her haunch, and runs a swab round the back of a shower cubicle or along a bench top or across the foetid sheets between which the homeowner — God, what sort of people submit to this intrusion? — sweats and writhes and drools and dribbles each centrally heated night. Miss Science bungs the resultant swab onto a petri dish, and whoa, it's suddenly the Amazon jungle. Streptococci sprout from the dish like saplings. Oh look, a leprosy flower, a thicket of legionnaire's, greeblies and threats. Be alarmed, be very alarmed, your house is filthy. And above all do not for one moment stop to think.

Do not reflect that no one ever, in the whole of human history, has died from licking their house. You could harvest the stuff that grows round your shower, dry it and sprinkle it on your breakfast cereal daily without ill effects. Indeed it would probably prove beneficial.

Are you getting enough fish oil? If not, be very alarmed. Your brain will shrivel to the size of a conker and you'll start liking motor sport. Are you prepared for the big one, or rather The Big One? Are your kids too fat? Are you a closet alcoholic? Complete this questionnaire. Have you got lumps? Check now. Do you love too much? Do you sag here, here and especially here? Got a six-pack? Women love a six-pack. (They like Scotch too, but they aren't getting any of mine.) Look there, no there, over there, see? No, not that fleet of drunk drivers revving their engines and lining up Grandma, but there, over there, where a swarm of rampant paedophiles is gathering in your suburb like wildebeest on an African plain. Have you planned for your retirement? Will you be reduced to eating coal? Will you be able to afford coal? The glaciers are going. Look, that brute is smoking a cigarette. Near me! Al Qaeda, Al Gore, does my bum look big in this, HN51 is just around the corner, not if but when, be alarmed alarmed alarmed.

None of this stuff comes to pass, of course. And if it does we rather enjoy the adversity. It sharpens the mettle. But that's not the point. The point is, why is so much effort made to spread alarm in the least alarming world in history?

Oh come on now, think. It's obvious. For one thing we expect to fear. Our programming requires it. But far more significantly it's a very useful emotion for authorities to exploit. If they suggest that there are lollipop eyes everywhere, we become timid and obedient. Fear renders us vulnerable to persuasion. Fear induces us to buy. Frighten the little children and they will be good.

It was a shed for our times.

latter of horses' hooves. The
. chapter of a 2000-year-old
orses of the Apocalypse. And
names are The, and Price, and
r those drumming hooves. Oh,
our neck.
rd us over the Cliff of Extinction
Jones, let us try to be calm and
read beasts. And who better to do
se readers of the contemporary tea
leaves, an ecc. st? So, regardless of expense — why husband money when the end of the world is at hand? — I hired an economist so freshly qualified from the University of the Internet that the ink was barely dry on his framed diploma. I wheeled him in and I sat him down and I grilled him.

Tell me, I shouted above the din of hooves, why the price of petrol is soaring like the lark. Why, every time I stop at the pumps, someone is up a ladder changing the price. It's killing me, Mr Economist. My car is not a luxury but a necessity. Without a car this town is uninhabitable. The mall where I worship is too distant to walk to. What's to become of my life, not to mention its associated style?

The economist shrugged.

Is there a shortage of oil, Mr Economist? I know that all the prosperity that I take as my right has grown from cheap energy, the energy stored long long ago when trillions of little sea creatures laid down their lives in the sedimentary rocks and kindly composted themselves into 91 octane petrol. I know too that we have been profligate with those creatures' remains, that for a century or so we have spent them as casually as Mrs Beckham spends dollars. I know too, we all know, naggingly, that oil is finite, that the day of no oil must come, but it isn't now, is it? Are we scraping, at this very moment, in 2008, the last smears of the dead from the bottom of the oil barrel?

The economist shook his head.

In that case, have we reached what the sandal-wearers and bearded women have been warning us about? Have we reached Peak Oil, the beginning of the end which is worse than the end itself because it marks the start of a shrinking and dwindling that can lead only to war on a global scale, as the billions of poor who have nothing to lose take on the millions of rich who are unwilling to give? Have we reached that point?

Again the economist slowly shook that great sagacious head.

So if, right now, there is no actual shortage of oil, if there is enough for everyone who wants it to get it, why is the price rising so cruelly and swiftly? Are you going to blame that amorphous entity 'the market', the point where buyer meets seller?

The economist nodded, vigorously, eager to confirm that I had struck the nail unerringly on its bright little metal head.

Then let us consider the oil companies, I said, like BP, or Royal Dutch Shell. They sell petrol. But they also mine for oil. They suck it from the sands or the seabed and they refine it and they pipe it into those great sausage-like tankers that crawl about our roads like potential infernos on wheels and they deliver it to petrol stations that they themselves own in order to sell it to us. Have I got that wrong?

The wise head shook.

So when we buy that oil it is being sold for the very first time. In other words we are the market. And yet we have no power to bargain. Only today at my local BP station I told the man I'd pay $1.50 a litre and no more. He laughed. He fell about laughing.

The economist chuckled.

Well, I have done some research, my money-understanding friend, and found that in the first three months of this year, and that's before the price really took off, BP and Shell made a combined profit of about $18 billion. That's $18,000 million in approximately 90 days. That's $200 million a day, or in excess of $8 million an hour, assuming they work around the clock and on Sundays, which at that sort of hourly rate they probably do.

The oil company costs have not risen. So are they charging us more simply because they can? Or is there some other explanation?

The economist opened his mouth at last to speak but at that moment hooves clattered through the roof of my dwelling and suddenly, much to my relief, we arrived at the end of the.

Confess that brolly

Let me begin the year with some advice to the young: confess your sins. Confess them before someone finds them out and confesses them for you. You may imagine that your sins are unspeakable, but you are wrong. Speak the unspeakable and you will be surprised what the world will forgive. Have courage.

And lest you think I am all words and no action, I shall haul a truth from the murk of my depravity and hold it up for you to gawp at: until recently I owned a golf umbrella.

Go on. Biff the rotten fruit of derision. You can biff nothing that I haven't biffed myself in the torture of my guilt.

I knew my umbrella was a golf umbrella because it was enormous. Why golfers need enormous umbrellas I have no idea, but then I also have no idea why golfers need umbrellas at all. Playing golf at any time is a cry for help. Playing golf in the rain is a cry for rubber cutlery and a jacket that buckles at the back.

Yet in the strange inverted world that we have made for ourselves, professional golfers are thought close to God. They have acolytes called caddies. Caddies are anonymous bag-toters, expendable beasts of burden. Except, that is, for the caddy to Mr T. Woods, the pope of golf. His caddy has become a celebrity. I don't believe I know a sadder fact.

When the heavens have the temerity to rain on a professional golfer — and I fully expect the Royal and

Ancient to sort out that little anomaly soon — the caddy holds the giant umbrella over his master but not over himself. The scene resembles Good King Wenceslas in reverse.

In order to play his shot, the master has to step forth into the pitiless drizzle. Does the caddy take momentary shelter under the brolly? He does not. He holds the brolly over the clubs.

I don't know how I acquired my golf umbrella. I obviously didn't buy it. It was emblazoned with the name of a bank. I am not in the habit of stealing from banks — the reverse is closer to the truth — so I presume the bank gave it to me. Perhaps they wanted to thank me for not having my overdraft with them.

But there it stood in my garage on Boxing Day, along with me, my car and my dog, all of whom were heading forth into torrential rain. I looked at the umbrella and I thought why not and I tossed it into the boot.

When all goes well, an umbrella is the roof that walks with you. And there is something sweet in standing in a cylinder of drought amid walls of water. It's like an inverted womb.

But umbrellas are bad at wind. Spectacularly anarchically bad. And on these islands, rain without wind is about as common as a television newsreader without an autobiography.

The wind was at my back. I hoisted the brolly like a shouldered rifle and bounced along the track, my strides lengthened like a moonwalker's strides. It was agreeable. I like elemental forces and here was an elemental force harnessed.

The track is cut into the hillside. And it writhes. At the first writhing the wind bounced off the bank and gathered instantly under the umbrella's hood. Suddenly I was wrestling with a mushroom on a stick. Had I been in reflective mode I would promptly have invented the sailboat and the parachute and written the score for *Mary Poppins*. But I was not in reflective mode. I was in wrestling mode. I wrestled and whoa, the mushroom detumesced.

Now the wind and rain came at me from the front. I held the brolly before me as a Roman infantryman held his shield. I was pushing against the sky. I progressed not like a moonwalker but like a walker on some planet with ferocious gravity. Below the umbrella my jeans went unprotected into the horizontal rain. It felt like walking in wet carpet. I peeped around my shield to see what I was walking towards and I caught a glimpse of misery. I called my dog and turned.

Instantaneously the wind recaptured the brolly. The cloth tried to restrain the sky. It was momentarily a struggling, swelling, writhing bicep of air, then the bicep flipped, the cloth tore from the spokes and I was holding a wrecked thing, a was, a flapping dead swan.

I threw the golf brolly over the cliff. Let the world eat it. Let the world rot it. The rain lashed at my head. And I ran with my dog, ran with the wind, ran in my jeans of carpet, puddle-stamping, sodden and joyful, my sin behind me and gone. It was lovely. Do the same, you young people, do the same. Throw away the golf umbrella of guilt. Run shriven in the rain. And have a happy new year.

Good stuff

Are you up for a miracle? Good. Take a quart of fresh cream. Resist the urge to drink it straight from the bottle or to tip it onto chocolate cake to make a sludge of glory. I know that's a lot to ask, but today we're aiming high.

Shake the cream. Shake it till your arm aches. When the miracle happens, you'll sense it. Open your bottle of cream. Floating there you'll find a nugget of pale and squidgy gold. People call it butter. I call it a miracle. Professor Rod Jackson, who is an epidemiologist from Auckland, calls it poison.

Few words sound as good as the word butter. It sounds fat. It sounds lazy. It sounds indulgent. And because it sounds good we have attached it to good things. Buttercups are the richest of spring flowers. Hold a buttercup under your chin and your face is bathed in reflected gold.

To butter someone up is to ply him with flattery and gifts until his defences crumble. Butter, you see, is a seducer. Would anyone have watched *Last Tango in Paris* if Marlon Brando had reached for the low-fat spread? Butter is sensuous.

And consider butterflies. We hate most insects because we know they'll inherit the Earth. We know that ants and cockroaches watched the dinosaurs come and go. We know that flies have fed on the dung of pterodactyls and the rotting flesh of mammoths. And we know that insects will be thriving when the human race is long gone. So we resent them. We give them harsh names and we point ferocious aerosols at them, with the sole exception of butterflies. Butterflies seem threatless, vulnerable, pretty and good. We love them. Though I expect Professor Jackson swats them.

When I was a child my mother made biscuits. They were earnest oaten things, just lumps of roughage. But I knew how to make them good. I made butter sandwiches with them. When my young teeth closed on the biscuits, the butter curled out from between them. I have only to close my eyes now and I can taste it.

Imagine sweet corn without butter, crumpets without butter, asparagus without butter, France without butter. I have been rude about the French but even I acknowledge they can cook. Their sauces are pleasure on a spoon. And all French sauces are based on butter. In the ever-rolling now of life, butter is joy.

And Professor Jackson is a killjoy. 'There's no reason,' he says, 'to use butter in anything.' Wrong, Prof, wrong. There is a single irrefutable reason. I like the stuff.

Professor Jackson hates it with a messianic passion. 'All the good things have been taken out . . . ,' he says. 'They've just left the poison.'

Poison is a strong word, Prof, and here it's a false one. Poison's only purpose is to kill. Butter's first purpose is to please. And as sage old Kingsley Amis said, and as I never tire of repeating, 'No pleasure is worth giving up for two more years in a rest home.'

Your work, Prof, has blinded you to a distinction. Peering down your microscope you've lost sight of the difference between longevity and living. You know from your research that butter clogs arteries and that clogged arteries kill. You know your physiology. And your concern is only with keeping the physiology going as long as possible, 'as though to breathe were life'. How long is it since you read Tennyson, Prof?

My mother is 85. Apart from during the war, she has eaten butter every day of her life. And wouldn't you know it, she has heart problems. But butter didn't cause the heart problems. Being 85 caused them. The body runs down, Prof, and then it stops. When it stops matters far less than what it gets up to before it stops. Living does not need to be an Everest-climbing, parapenting, swashbuckling rodeo ride. It can be a quiet domestic bobbing on a gentle swell of ups and down. But those ups and downs are the pleasures and pains of being alive. And one of the little pleasures is butter.

I have just learnt that here in New Zealand margarine was once forbidden by law. But that golden age ended in 1972 and now Prof Jackson and his fellow busybodies want us to live as long as, say, the Japanese do. They tut over our mortality rates with a frisson of virtuous horror and they point the finger at butter and its sister pleasures. They are wrong. It doesn't matter if the Japanese live longer than we do. It's not a competition. And one slice of toast with butter thick enough to leave tooth marks is worth a wrinkled decade of rice and fish. Be off with you, Prof. Leave me alone.

The blades of prophecy

It had to happen. I knew it had to happen. And now it has happened. My only regret is that I didn't announce that it would happen. I thought of announcing it a while ago — yes, yes, I did, really and truly, cross my heart and hope to be spit-roasted by a bloke with cloven hooves and a tail like a flexible spear — but I just thought to myself, no, it can wait because it won't happen for a while yet and right now I've got more important things to say. But it's happened sooner than I expected and now no one is going to believe that I knew it was going to happen and thus I have missed my chance to become a prophet.

It would be nice to be a prophet — devotees handing me choice morsels, the faithful prostrating themselves so that I get an unobstructed view of the cricket, disciples tailing me with notebooks desperate to scribble down my every utterance in the hope of getting edited into the eventual *Big Book of the Truth*, a book that would just go on selling as the Harry Bloody Potters came and went like autumn leaves.

I'd be a real prophet, of course, without any of that obscurantist Nostradamus stuff. You wouldn't catch me prophesying that 'a lion shall arise in the east and its name shall be Hrtlr and it shall make smoke in the mountains of desperation'. No, I'd be utterly forthright. I'd say things like 'China will invade Siberia before 2020 because China will have run out of oil and water, and because China will have more and bigger guns than anyone else' or 'The dollar will fall below 70 US cents by the end of 2007' or 'They'll carry on taking drugs in the Tour de France and most other sports because it helps them win and anyway no one minds much because people like watching freaks'. All of these statements happen to be true, of course, but they're so obvious that they don't count as prophecy.

Plenty of people try a bit of prophecy, but they make the mistake of going straight for the big one, usually the end of the world. This brings easy fame and dollars at the outset, but as the predicted date nears you can see them buying dark glasses and plane tickets for South America.

Prophecy isn't a talent. It's just a technique. All it requires is a bit of thinking. Then you've just got to ignore the clamour of the short-term loudmouths, stick to your guns — whatever that means — and you're away. Consider the Sage of Omaha, the endlessly dreary and even more endlessly wealthy Mr Buffett. Back in about 1960 he had a quick squiz around the suburbs of Omaha, noticed that people liked buying things that worked, realised that human nature wouldn't change, stuck his few dollars into companies that made things that worked, and left those dollars where they were. Prophecy's open to anyone.

But I do regret not prophesying what has just come true. I think you'd have been impressed and I'm not yet beyond wanting to impress people. The prophecy concerned shaving.

My father's razor had a mechanism at its head that opened like Batman's car. Into it you screwed a blade with two edges, both of them lethal. If you laid the blade on a flat surface you could never pick it up. That blade defined manhood.

Well manhood's gone, replaced by David Beckham. With manhood went the old razor blade because David Beckham just couldn't cope with the danger. In came the twin-blade safety razor.

Advertisers illustrated its betterness by inventing the evasive follicle. This follicle ducked a bit as the first blade came through, then raised its head once it thought the danger was past, only for the second blade to surprise it. The evasive follicle was shown only in cartoon form because no actual follicle ever behaved like that. But the twin blade swept the market for the simple reason that two just had to be better than one.

What's better than two? Inevitably it wasn't long before the three-blade razor arrived, its virtues illustrated by a cartoon follicle that ducked like a tree in a storm. Would we swallow it? We swallowed it.

But it was only when the Gillette Quattro popped up a year or two ago that I thought of a bit of grooming prophecy. Within a year, I said to myself, there will be five blades. But I didn't say it in print, so I don't expect you to believe me. And now, of course, it's happened. I've seen a five-blade razor advertised.

Will we reach six blades, seven, 10? Probably. Though I'm not prophesying them. My prophecy, and pay attention now, is that before the end of 2008 some manufacturer will spend billions of dollars in an effort to convince us punters that the very best sort of razor in the world is actually, after all, a single blade. You read it here first.

Sheikh Yawallet

Oil at $100 a barrel is bad news for deer.

The front page of *The Press* last week showed a photo of a red deer stag that appeared to be sleeping but was actually dead. It had been shot. The bloke who shot it was standing heroically behind it. He was fat. His mother would no doubt describe him as big-boned, and he might tell you his problem was glandular, but to me he just looked like a fat slob. He was also a prince of Qatar.

If I were Qatari he could probably do nasty things to me for calling him a slob. But I am not Qatari and I have no plans to become one, so I'll stick with the word. His double chins had double chins.

Imagine a Middle Eastern princeling and you see him in one of those graceful white robes that they favour when chatting with Condoleezza about the purchase of another squadron of F1-11s. But Sheikh Yawallet was on holiday. His holiday clothes consisted of a pair of trackpants and an XXXXOS polo shirt that did him no aesthetic favours.

In contrast with Sheikh Yawallet, the stag was sleek and beautiful. It also had impressive antlers. In the wild those antlers would have given it mating rights, but in the strange world of international shooting, they just made the stag a desirable target. Anyone who shot it would earn over 500 International Safari Club points, and thereby qualify for membership of the Platinum 500 Club. What members of that club do when they meet, I don't know. Boast, I suppose.

But anyway, because of those antlers Bambi was transported by truck to a game park near exotic Timaru, and Sheikh Yawallet was transported by private jet from the Middle East to the same game park.

They met some time last year. Bambi, apparently, had an 'eat out of your hand' personality. And Sheikh Yawallet, armed only with a high-powered rifle, a Range Rover and a packed lunch, shot it.

At which point out came the champagne, the congratulations and the Nikon. Flunkies arranged the dead stag in a decorous posture, then winched Dead-eye Dick out of the vehicle, posed him behind the victim, and took a series of snaps that at this very moment are probably boring the Qatari royal family to a coma.

The whole business invites a host of questions, the first and most obvious of which is why. Why should Sheikh Yawallet have flown halfway round the world to shoot a semi-tame deer? The equally obvious answer is that he could afford to. He was born on top of a society that sits on top of an oil field. As a result he has been the lifelong beneficiary of a torrent of cash.

But why didn't he stay at home and shoot camels? Camels are indigenous to the Gulf and the locals have found numerous uses for them, including racing. I've seen racing camels in training. A malnourished Pakistani infant is strapped to each beast as a jockey and then the camels are set to run across the desert, their necks stretching ahead of them like geese reaching for apricots. Owners and trainers follow in air-conditioned Nissan Pathfinders and billows of dust.

If you ignore the child jockeys, who are discarded

when they grow to weigh more than a couple of stone, camel racing is indistinguishable from horse racing. And just as we don't shoot horses for sport, so Arabs don't shoot camels. Instead they come here to shoot deer. The reason is antlers.

Antlers represent masculinity. Their only purpose is fighting. Big antlers give a stag supremacy and the right to mate with does. Did the sheikh want to mate with does? Let's be charitable and presume not. So why did he want to kill the deer? The only possible answer is a notion that had its heyday when human beings lived in caves. The notion is that if you kill a powerful beast you acquire some of its potency. The idea is primitive, superstitious and fetishistic. And it's big business.

The story was in the paper because a squabble has arisen over Bambi's semen. Apparently semen can be extracted from a stag's testicles even after death, and Bambi's semen is valuable because it contains the blueprint for big antlers. But an administrative bungle meant that the semen was wrongly attributed, so its owners can't sell it for what it's worth. And what's it's worth is multibucks because with oil approaching $100 a barrel there's going to be a lot more sheikhs wanting to come here and shoot Bambi's offspring in order to feel like men.

Six in the morning

Six in the morning and it is raining. Three hours from now I shall drive my dog over the hill. When I pull up outside the vet's surgery the dog's mood will slump. He does not forget. But I'll coax him through the door and the vet will give him a sedative injection in the scruff of the neck. Then we'll leave and the dog will be delighted. He will have no idea that we are just going for a walk on the beach while the sedative takes effect. Dogs inhabit now.

Perhaps 20 minutes later we'll return. The dog will be drowsy, and re-entering the surgery will not alarm him. My presence will be enough to reassure him that all manner of things are well. I'll lift his 30-something kilos onto a table of stainless steel and he will pay little attention while the vet anaesthetises him. And when he's out, with a breathing tube thrust down his throat, and all the qualities in abeyance that make him my dog, I shall leave him. I will want to stay but I expect the vet will want me to leave. And then the vet will take a scalpel and cut open the dog's stomach and fluids will pour out and within minutes the vet will make the decision whether the dog will live or die.

Ten days ago I noticed that the dog was growing plump. I like my dogs to be lean so they can run. We do miles every day. I reduced his food a little. Two days later he seemed plumper. That upward curve of the gut to the haunch had gone, the curve that announces a fit young dog. Another two days and it was clear that something was wrong. He was happy and energetic and still eating well, but his stomach felt taut with fluid, like a bladder of warm wine. I took him to the vet. The vet took a blood sample from his leg, then drew a syringe of fluid from the swollen gut. It was the colour of pinot noir.

I nursed the dog through the weekend. He took little nursing. Though slowed by the bulk of his gut, he took joy from all the things that dogs take joy from, beaches, hills, food, touch, other dogs and the endless sensory world.

Yesterday the vet rang. Analysis of the samples showed that his liver and kidneys were fine. But blood was leaking into his gut. The cause was most likely to be a tumour. If it was on the spleen and only the spleen, then that would be good. An adult dog can live a fine life with no spleen. But if the cancer was more widespread, well, the vet could only find out by opening him up. I booked the dog in for surgery today, two and a half hours from now. I have told the vet that if the cancer is terminal, inoperable, he should not wake the dog up.

The dog is about six years old. Four years ago a friend sent him to me from Australia as a gift. The dog had had several owners in the first two years of his life and their ignorance warped his nature. He was unsocialised and aggressive. In the first days I had him he bit a visitor, bailed others up against the fence. He charged other dogs.

But he was a rewarding dog to train and slowly he came good. Aggression in dogs is only fear pushed up a level. These days I can take him anywhere and if he is alarmed he looks at me and I tell him it is all okay and that's enough for him.

And today he may die, in a few hours. He has no sense of dread. When I finish writing this I shall take him for a walk as I do every morning, and then I'll give him a bone as I do every morning. He'll take it outside to chew it in the rain. A little later I'll call him to come to the car and he will be delighted by the surprise of another walk. And I'll take him to the vet.

It does not seem fair. But fairness is a human notion. It is not written into the contract of existence. What happens happens. The arc of his life may be cut off when it is at its height. Words and money are as impotent as prayers.

As I lay him on the vet's table he will simply trust me. And I'll say something into his ear and I'll kiss him and I hope that as he sinks towards sleep that there's enough of him left for his tail to slap weakly against the stainless steel. And I hope I'll see him alive again, later this wet morning.

For your reading entertainment

'For your reading entertainment,' said the air hostess over the public address system, 'you will find a copy of our in-flight magazine in the seat pocket in front of you. This is complimentary and you are welcome to take it with you.'

Well, I did just what you would have done. I dived into the seat pocket, rummaged a bit, came up with the sick bag and filled it. What else could one do after a chunk of language like that?

Where shall I start? Let's start with the air hostess, who isn't an air hostess any more. She's a flight attendant. Neither is the right term to describe her job, but on balance I prefer air hostess. The word hostess implies a party. It derives from the days when flying was thought glamorous.

There was once a group called the jet set. Everyone knew what they looked like. They wore polo-neck sweaters and miniskirts, often simultaneously. Tanned, rich and beautiful, they swigged champagne and had unlimited sex and were greatly envied. They were the international party people. They were also probably mythical.

But I'm old enough to remember non-mythical parties on planes. For three years in the 1980s I lived in Canada. I must have crossed the Atlantic a dozen times and I never got off the plane sober. The cause was smoking. The back 10 rows or so of the aircraft were designated smoking seats. But there were always more smokers than seats, so those who'd got marooned in conformityville at the pilot's end all migrated to the back after take-off and stood in the aisles and smoked and drank and laughed and drank and had a party and got in the way of proper people wanting to use the lavatories and it was lovely.

Smoking on planes is long gone, of course, because, according to the official announcement, 'Smoking's a hazard'. 'So's flying, my dear,' I always mutter. 'So's living, for God's sake.' But it doesn't do any good.

When smoking went, the fun went with it. I haven't been on a party plane since. Now we sit like beasts bound for the abattoir and instead of being hosted by air hostesses we are attended by flight attendants.

The term flight attendant suits the times. It is sexually neutral — unlike most flight attendants I've met — and corporate pale. It offends nobody and conjures no mental image. It's an example of the wet flannel language of this bland and frightened age.

The pleasure I used to get from standing at the back of planes drinking and smoking and laughing with flesh and blood has been replaced by officially sanctioned pleasure in the form of an 'entertainment centre'. This consists of a console that I can't operate but that kids intuitively master, poor things, and a screen housed in the seat back. Sixty years ago George Orwell saw the screen as a threat to human happiness. Orwell was no fool.

A screen offers the same sort of pleasure as a baby's dummy. It is passive and bloodless. It requires nothing of you but the cessation of mental effort. Unlike a raucous, hazardous, smoke-enshrouded back-of-the-plane beano, watching a screen is predictable and solitary. You contribute nothing but your attention. The screen's entire purpose is to pacify you while the airline makes a profit. I don't want to be pacified. Nor do I want to be entertained.

Which brings me back to the opening announcement. Jeremy Clarkson said that the worst word in the world is beverage. I think it's complimentary. Complimentary is a corporate synonym for free. They use it because it's longer and it carries a hint of flattery.

Everything complimentary is tat. That includes every airline magazine, or in-flight magazine, as they like to call them. They're all identical. The editorial text is indistinguishable from the ads. It's travel gush: tune in to the vibrant rhythms of the Caribbean; find your perfect romantic hideaway in unspoilt Vanuatu; live it up with the friendly locals in Shagalot, Kentucky. A tsunami of mendacious gloss. Nothing within the magazine's covers bears the least relation to reality. It's one more aspect of the world of corporate delusion.

Nevertheless it's a magazine. And call me a know-all if you like, but if I'm told that there's a magazine in front of me, I know what to do with it. The airline, however, doesn't believe that I could possibly be so independently informed. They feel obliged to tell me not only that the magazine's for reading, but that it's for my reading entertainment.

And there you have it, the world of today as plain as plain. A world that treats us like babies. A world that tells us how to be and what to do and what to think about what we do. A patronising world. A conformist world without savour. A world that exists to brainwash, to pacify us all the way back to babyhood, to delude us, and to make a profit. Battle it. Let's smoke.

Now listen up, America

A friend in Florida has told me that my column has little influence on American politics. He is a good friend and before lunch he sometimes talks sense, so let us suppose he is right. Let us imagine, absurd though it may seem, that no words of mine will affect the coming US presidential election. What should I do?

The question is rhetorical. 'Yea, though the prophet shall stand alone in the desert,' says Chapter 1, verse 1 of St Paul's Letter to the Bibulous, 'yet he shall talk to the sand.'

Dear sand, it is a vital election. The 20th century was the American century. But the 21st century is boarding a one-way flight to Beijing.

Throughout my life America has been the world's big brother. It had zest, energy, success. It made mistakes, and bad ones, but that was just because big brothers have to make big decisions.

Big brothers are umbrellas under which little brothers shelter. And now the American umbrella is looking tattered. Spokes are protruding through the cloth. When the breeze rises, the cloth flaps. It would be nice, but wrong, to blame George Bush. He has presided over decline but that is because he is the sort of emperor that empires in decline elect.

There is no reason to hate President Bush. There is every reason to pity him. Would you want to take on the job that your father did poorly and do it worse?

Would you want to have been promoted beyond your ability? Would you want to lack the self-knowledge to recognise that you have been promoted beyond your ability? Would you want to wake at midnight to the unshakable knowledge that you will go down in history as a dolt? Would you want every idea in your head to have been put there by somebody else? And would you want to find your native language hard? Would you want to feel, every time you started a sentence, that the journey to the full stop was like a steeplechase from hell, the hurdles wrapped with razor wire, and the water jump swirling with piranhas?

No one could enjoy being President George. But plenty of people have enjoyed George being president. People who drill for oil or who manufacture weapons. And people who hover around the back rooms of Washington like parasitic wasps waiting for the chance to dart into the president's ear and implant a verbal egg, an egg that will enter the bloodstream to hatch and feast and grow and emerge a month or two later from the host's mouth, albeit a little mangled.

These people will soon lose George. By virtue of the wise constitution he will return to Texas, where wealthy harridans will invite him to dinner to tell stories of his favourite executions. Oh, how they will laugh. Oh, how their long teeth will twinkle in the candlelight. Oh, how their corn-fed bellies will swell against the gauze and satin. But the rest of the world won't know. Texas will have George and George will have Texas and that will be that. The world will be moving on.

How soon the 20th century ends will depend on the next president. It is a vital choice. And we all know in our guts who America should choose.

It is not Mike Huckabee. He is an evangelical preacher. Those words should debar anyone from any post requiring independent thought.

It is not John McCain. He was imprisoned by the Vietcong. He remains imprisoned by the 20th century. For all his alleged maverick qualities, we've seen him before. We've seen his hair on the grandfather figure in every American sitcom.

It is not Hillary Clinton. She is her husband without the suave sexual charm. And her husband without the suave sexual charm was very little indeed. Hillary weeps on demand. She stands for the acquisition of power, and that is all. Tap her and she rings like a hollow tree. Owls could nest in her. I hope they do.

It is Barack Obama. He is blackish, which is probably about as black as you can be to stand a chance of being elected. He is youngish. He is handsome. And he rings a note that used to be America's note. It's a note of fresh hope.

I have no idea what he stands for and it doesn't matter. Policy is nothing. There are plenty of people with good brains but bad faces to make policy. A presidential election is not about policy. It is the politics of perceived personality.

People have always followed leaders for how they seem rather than for what they think. And how Obama seems is good and different. America needs desperately to be good and different. It could renew, albeit briefly, its lease on empire. Go on, Americans, be brave and choose him.

There, I'm done. And when Barack Obama is taking his oath on the steps of the White House, I shall ring Florida and say, 'See?'

I took the costly wine

I took the costly wine along. Really, I did. Though it was only a casual invitation to dinner at a friend's house, and though there was nothing special about the food or the guests, and though the costly wine had been a gift from an organisation, a gift handed over with the sort of reverence with which Mary handed over the baby Jesus to one of the wise men for dandling, I took the bottle along with me. Are there no limits to my generosity?

Yes, there are severe limits to my generosity. Indeed I am confident of being less generous than you are. I give only to animal charities and then not as much as I can afford, and I walk whistling past beggars, smug with self-interest, my conscience giving not even the tiniest of clicks.

Had I bought the bottle it would have set me back, according to my one acquaintance who knows about wine, or pretends to, which is usually enough in this credulous world where people are awe-struck by any claim to expertise, somewhere north of $50.

When I say north of $50 I am quoting. I would never say north of anything unless I were giving directions. I strive to avoid the financial euphemisms that plague us. We are so shy of money, and so reverential. Money is the glowing godhead whose name must not be spoken openly. For the lord my dosh is a jealous god.

Nevertheless I had deemed the wine too good to drink and I had unconsciously reserved it for a very special occasion. But you know how it is with very special occasions. They just don't happen. I am too old and too remote from family to be invited to weddings, and though good drinking happens at funerals, no one takes a bottle to a funeral. It would smack of honesty, and that would never do.

So the very special occasion persisted in not cropping up, and the bottle on the kitchen shelf began to irritate me, reminding me of the flatness of my world, its lack of Everestish peaks. I dwell in the Plains of the Ordinary, and the Mountains of Distinction lie beyond the far horizon.

Though if truth be told, no one has very special occasions. Even the most glittering events, the Queen's garden party, the Oscars bash, the thrash on board the billionaire's Caribbean yacht, are all as dull as a ditch. Take away the paparazzi cameras, the press attention, the sense of anticipation and you are left with every party you have ever attended: dull people talking about the weather and thinking about sex.

So in the end my reason for taking the costly wine to this mundane event was that I wanted to be rid of it. It spoke to me too grimly and too much.

But I still wanted credit for my generosity. I made sure I was last to arrive. I entered with the bottle held in front of me like a talisman of my virtue. 'Look,' I said, 'fifty smackers worth of wine.'

'Ooooh,' said the throng and chattered excitedly. For gatherings are sad little events. We think somehow they should transcend the normal. But they don't because no event alters the normality of the people, their reticence, their lack of ooomph, honesty and sparkle. Only booze can do that, which is why all events feature booze. The price of the booze is irrelevant. All that matters is its alcoholic content, which prises people open, causes indiscretion, and invests the mundane with a glittering halo of drug-induced tinsel.

Then one man suggested we should do a blind wine-tasting, to see if we could distinguish the costly plonk from the cheap. Another man offered to act as sommelier. He hated wine, he said. He drank only tequila and Coke.

Giggling, we all left the kitchen while he prepared three glasses, two of the sort of $6.99 red that we all bring to parties and one of the priceless nectar. In we trooped, one after another, to sip, blind-folded, from all three glasses and give each of the wines a mark out of 10. Some people took it terribly seriously. They swirled the glass, sniffed its odours, sipped the wine, spun it about the mouth, spat it out and rinsed the tongue with water before sampling the next glass. Others just drank.

And the result? You want to know the result? You don't think you can guess? You really believe there may be something in this wine-buff malarkey? You believe that a wine may exist that transcends the ordinary, that lands on the tongue like angels coupling? You believe, indeed, that the whole business of wine appreciation is more than just a middle-class disguise for the usefulness of a drug that gets us through the tedium of social gatherings? You do? Well, you should have been there.

The marks awarded by seven ignorant but honest tasters were added together. My bottle scored worst.

Seldomly

'Seldomly,' said the cricket commentator. 'You seldomly see . . .'

I didn't hear what it was that you seldomly saw because I was laughing. 'Ha ha,' I was saying, 'you illiterate former sportsman who are still hanging around the only world you have ever known because everything else is terrifying, ha ha. Seldomly! Oh, come on. It's the sort of error a child would make.'

And it is. It is exactly the sort of error a child would make. Children learn patterns. They learn, for instance, to make a past tense by adding -ed to a verb. So they say I runned, I thinked. The commentator did something similar. Seldom is an adverb. Most adverbs end in -ly. The commentator sensed the need for an adverb and, without doing any conscious analysis, added the -ly. 'Seldomly,' he said. 'Ha ha,' I said.

So the commentator spoke like a child. And I reacted like a child. My ha ha was a crow of triumph. 'Oh Mr Commentator,' it said, 'you got the language wrong and I noticed that you got it wrong and I would not get it wrong myself, so I am better than you are. I'm the king of the castle and you're the dirty rascal. Ha ha ha ha ha ha.' My reaction was uglier than his error.

Language must communicate. That is what it exists to do. If it does not transfer a notion from one head to another then it is merely noise. And a lot of language is just that. It is vibrations on the air, as meaningful as the hiss of surf.

Many words spouted by consultants and politicians, for example, communicate nothing. The speaker wants to be heard, or to be elected, or to be paid, but has nothing to say. His words leave a mental mist. He hopes that his status will daunt you and me from challenging his language. Or that you and I will presume the failure lies at our end rather than his.

If language succeeds in communicating then it is doing its job and there is no such thing as right and wrong. But a glance at the letters page suggests that something different is going on. It suggests that there are rules to language and people get upset when they are broken.

Rules are always popular. They offer something to cling to, chunks of driftwood in the chaotic ocean of now. It is easier to cling to rules than to swim independently. How else, for example, could thousands of apparently decent people have assisted in mass murder at Auschwitz? Their defence is always that they were only following orders, obeying the rules. What people don't say is that they like rules. Rules make things simple.

But the rules of language are not rules. Over a couple of thousand years the English language has moved seamlessly from something Germanic and inflected to the almost uninflected global language of today. It has done so in defiance of all rules except one. That rule is the need to communicate. All other apparent rules have dissolved as the years have gone by. They have proved to be only conventions. And conventions change.

But people fear change as much as they fear the chaotic ocean. So they cling to the conventions, and knowing those conventions becomes a badge of merit. Oh look at him, he doesn't know who from whom. Oh, look at that apostrophe in sausage's. Oh look, the commentator said seldomly. Has he a brain?

Well now, in English the distinction between who and whom no longer serves a purpose. Word order dictates meaning, so we don't need whom in order to make meaning clear. In evolutionary terms whom is a dying duck. In 30 years it will be a dead duck. And though we pedants cherish it, the same is true of the apostrophe. We would be better off without it, and we soon will be.

Language looks after itself. Nothing we can do will prevent its evolution. Evolutionary theory dictates that what is linguistically useful will survive. What is not will wither. If the language is in decline, it is only because we are. And sometimes it is tempting to think that we are.

The distinction between may and might, for example, is both precise and useful. 'A bottle of beer may have saved the man's life' does not mean the same as 'A bottle of beer might have saved the man's life'. In the first sentence the victim is alive and well. In the second he's dead as mutton. And yet that useful distinction is becoming lost. For how often do even professional journalists distinguish between may and might? Seldomly, I'm afraid.

Manila

8.30 a.m. on a Tuesday morning and Manila's impossible. Or at least this bit of it is, though I'm not sure quite what bit this is. Twelve million people inhabit this city and most of them seem to have gathered here, right outside my hotel at an intersection and jeepney stop.

Jeepneys are good to look at, bad to ride. They derive, I am told, from American Jeeps left over after the Second World War, but they have evolved into distinctive beasts like shrunken Mack trucks with a fat-nosed diesel engine and chrome bodywork flamboyantly decorated. Passengers sit up in the cab with the vest-and-jandals driver, or on benches in the back. Air-conditioning is supplied by window-sized holes. When the rain comes, as it does fiercely and suddenly and often, sheets of plastic are pegged over the holes and the interior becomes a humidor.

Jeepneys are mid-range transport, between the tricycle taxis, with their sidecars and underpowered motorbikes, and buses as the West knows buses, only dirtier. And noisier. For Manila is noise and noise is Manila. There isn't a scrap of air that isn't constantly shunted, shifted, buffeted by noise, by engines, voices, slappings, bangs and screams. When priests here speak of the peace of God the congregation must sigh with disbelief.

At the jeepney stop a tiny man blows ferocious consecutive blasts on his whistle, waves jeepneys towards him, blocks them with a raised palm, shouts at the drivers, scuttles hither and thither in his jandals and his soiled green T-shirt, and the drivers ignore him.

What controls the jeepneys is the free market. Every driver is out for himself, nosing ahead if he can, battling through what is close to gridlock. The faint-hearted get nowhere. And every space between vehicles is filled by pedestrians, flowing like water through cracks and crevices, rounding static obstructions such as the umbrella mender who squats on the pavement by a pile of those thin articulated metal struts that keep an umbrella taut and for which I know no name.

The heat is murderous, the humidity worse. Stray dogs keep to the shade and I withdraw to the air-con of a café and a glass of mango juice. The front page of the *Philippine Star* is moist to the touch and drenched with death. Muslim militants in the south have killed 14 Marines, beheading half of them. A ferry has gone down in a region I haven't heard of, taking 100 people with it. Two tricycle drivers in Quezon City have been shot dead for no apparent motive — they were unlikely to have been worth robbing — and last night in another of Manila's many constituent cities, a bus failed to stop. A woman passenger, whose stop it was, stood up to remonstrate. The driver ignored her. She started down the aisle, was seized by the arm, thrown back into her seat and told to empty her purse. Six gunmen had hijacked the bus. They robbed every passenger, forced the driver to park in a building site, shot him dead, ripped out the radio, slashed the tyres and disappeared into the urban night. Their crime was not extraordinary and will not be solved. This city will just absorb it. Already greater noises, new deaths, have overwhelmed it.

Like so many metropolises, Manila works a gravitational pull on the country around it. Hundreds of people every day leave their hot villages with their rice-paddies, coconuts and cock-fighting arenas, and head for the noise and dirt of the capital in the hope of riches. Most find only squalor, a shack at the back of a market perhaps where foul water drips from a standpipe and the stray cats prowl. But they stay, for they are in Manila and so in with a chance. And somehow, despite the heat and the crime and the corruption and the gulf between rich and poor and the ceaseless noise, they contrive to smile more and to seem more gentle than we do in the safe fat West.

Tell me, Sir Jim

'Would you mind elaborating on that answer a little?' said the journalist.

'Yeah,' said Sir Jim. 'Yeah.'

'You would mind?'

'Yeah,' said Sir Jim. 'Yeah.'

'Perhaps I should rephrase the question then,' said the journalist, 'though I did strive to put it as simply as I could in the first place, bearing in mind the notorious self-abuse that you and the other members of your band practised, or at least reportedly practised, in the late 1970s, which, frankly, is a period that I would rather forget, and one which I had almost managed to forget until you and your kind decided it was time to dust off your electric guitars and comb your remaining wisps of hair into something suggestive of teenage rebellion and return to the only area of your life in which you have ever met with any success, to wit the banging of drums and the thrashing of guitars and the recitation of lyrics that make the wails of a baby sound sophisticated in comparison.'

'Yeah,' said Sir Jim. 'Yeah.'

'Right then,' said the journalist, 'here we go. Do you consider reforming a band called Punko and the Spunks to be a fitting activity for a 61-year-old, a 61-year-old, moreover, who is now a knight of the realm, having been dubbed by Her Majesty for "services to music", which, in your case, is like knighting an iceberg for services to shipping, but let that pass?'

'Yeah,' said Sir Jim. 'Yeah.'

'Well,' said the journalist, 'could you please explain exactly why you and your fellow musicians — and I do hope you can hear the quotation marks around that last word — have decided to stage a reunion concert — and there's a set of quotation marks round that word too? Is it Viagra for a wilting ego, or a wish to rekindle the past, or an unconscious response to the zeitgeist that considers youth to be the only good, or have you simply run out of money to support the way of life to which you have become undeservedly accustomed?'

'Yeah,' said Sir Jim. 'Yeah.'

'Most illuminating,' said the journalist. 'But surely even you must have noticed that you are not alone in self-resurrection, following as you do in the footsteps of Led Bloody Zeppelin, the terrifyingly synthetic Spice Girls and half a dozen other long-defunct bands whose names I thankfully can't bring to mind right now. Does this therefore mean, in your opinion, if you have one, that over the next few years we are likely to see half the popular entertainers who have ever been idolised by hormone-drenched adolescents exhumed, buffed up a bit, strung like puppets and wheeled out to lip-sync to a medley of their mercifully forgotten hits? Will Elvis rise from the grave to thrust his fleshless pelvis?'

'Yeah,' said Sir Jim. 'Yeah.'

'God forfend,' said the journalist. 'But do you also seriously believe that your former fans, now older and supposedly wiser, now parents or grandparents even, will emerge from their snug villas in suburbia to shake their paunches and boogie on down, or whatever the current vernacular term may be, to the same stuff as excited them when they were barely out of nappies?'

'Yeah,' said Sir Jim. 'Yeah.'

'Tell me,' said the journalist, his tone rising half an octave, 'am I alone in considering that image of the future to be horrible in the extreme, and the inescapable moral conclusion to be terminally saddening? Am I alone, for example, in being appalled by the knowledge that a man recently paid $21,000 for a ticket to see Led Zeppelin? I should add that I was appalled not just because the dolt considered the experience to be worth that much money, but also because, despite being the sort of man he obviously was, the adult world had somehow seen fit to reward him with the money to indulge his folly.'

'Yeah,' said Sir Jim. 'Yeah.'

The journalist paused and looked about the press conference. Television cameras lined the walls. In front of the booze-raddled features of slumping Sir Jim, microphones were clustered like a bouquet of flowers. Fellow hacks were scribbling in their shorthand notebooks. The journalist stood and flung his notebook to the floor. 'Very well, then,' he said, and as he spoke his shoulders rose as though a yoke had been lifted from them, 'I renounce the world. I'm out of here. If you want me I can be found in the hermit's cave on the Mountain of Integrity. Goodbye.'

The journalist strode from the hall. The press conference fell silent.

'Pompous prat,' said Sir Jim, and everyone fell about laughing.

We

Christmas is now a dog-end in time's ashtray, and your New Year's resolutions have joined it. The only excitement still on the agenda is the holiday road toll. It's the principal story in a storyless time. Big questions have still to be answered. Will we better last year's toll? Will we perhaps set a record and clap ourselves on the metaphorical back with a metaphorical driving glove? Will we continue to misuse the pronoun 'we'?

Well, I won't. Once this article is written I shall take no interest in the holiday road toll except to grind my teeth and mutter whenever I hear it mentioned. And I shall continue to give the lie to the misuse of 'we' by making exactly the same contribution to the road toll as I have made these 20 years, which is nil, zero, zilch, no contribution. Not once have I killed. Not once have I died.

And before you leap to your feet and buy me a drink for being so very upstanding and community-minded and wonderfully safe safe safe, I would point out that unless you are visited by stupidity or bad luck, you will make exactly the same contribution to the road toll. As will everyone you know. And to be congratulated for neither killing nor dying, for being neither stupid nor unlucky, is to set the bar in the Congratulations High Jump at approximately ankle level.

Yet the voices of ostensible concern will continue to scream at us about dangers we have never had the least trouble avoiding. Don't drive when asleep or on the phone or drunk. Look five times at intersections. Wear a dozen seat belts while slowing down on country roads, because we're all in this together don't you know and we, the screaming voices, care about you oh so very much.

They don't care, of course. They just like to seem to care. They get an endorphin drenching from feeling that they're doing good. So if you want to make a belated resolution that is both achievable and wise, resolve to ignore all voices that misuse the pronoun 'we'.

We blew the World Cup. No, we didn't. You and I made exactly the same contribution to the World Cup as we have made these 20 years, which is nil, zero, zilch, no contribution.

This year we have broken all records for abusing our children. No, we haven't. You and I have made exactly the same contribution to child abuse as we have made these 20 years, which is nil, zero, zilch, no contribution.

If you find the use of 'we' too pervasive and irritating, one way to avoid it at this time of the year is to go on holiday. Where are you thinking of going? Lonely Planet guidebooks are all excited about Montenegro. It is the first new country for a while, says Lonely Planet, so it's sure to be fizzing.

Nice of them to recommend it. It gives us one place emphatically to avoid. Lonely Planet's recommendation guarantees that throughout the exciting year to come Montenegro will be swarming with the sort of people who buy Lonely Planet guidebooks. And why anyone when travelling should buy a guidebook, I have no idea.

The only charm of travel is the charm of the unexpected. Travel should take you to a bar where women sit on the floor plucking chickens while the resident snake-vendor sits whittling himself a new leg and his sister offers to sleep with you for your dentures.

You won't find that in Montenegro this year. Instead you'll find leisure-suited herds toting guidebooks from one must-see cultural disappointment to the next.

So where to go instead? Well, I recommend Bohmte.

Where?

Bohmte.

Bohmte in Germany?

Yes, Bohmte in Germany.

Why?

Because they're conducting a revolution as profound as the one they had a crack at in Paris in 1789. In 1789, as you may recall, they shouted Liberte, Egalite, Fraternite, sprinkled them with acute accents that I don't know how to find on my anglophonous computer, and biffed out the Ancien Regime. In Bohmte, they've biffed out the road rules.

In Bohmte's town centre there is now no distinction between footpath and roadway. There are no traffic lights, no stop signs, no speed limits, no one-way streets, no parking rules, no traffic cops, nothing. There are just gaps between buildings that you may choose to walk or drive along as you wish.

It's an anthropological experiment of the most interesting kind. Will liberty, equality, fraternity and concern for the welfare of others triumph, creating a city centre where cautiously crawling motorists defer politely to each other and to pedestrians, or will the streets turn anarchic and the road toll shoot for the sky? Well, it depends on how you see the human race.

All I will say is that shortly after the French Revolution, liberte, egalite, fraternite and all, they invented the guillotine.

Here's to fat Pavo

Had Pavarotti never existed I'd still think 'Nessun Dorma' was a Japanese campervan.

God knows what the song's about. Something to do with sleeping, I imagine, and probably, if I know anything about opera, romantic love. But I don't know anything about opera and anyway it doesn't matter. What matters is the singing.

Pavarotti wore a tuxedo the size of a marquee. His eyes were huge and dark and soft. Despite his bulk there was something of the baby about him. He played on that. Women melted. He was simultaneously the adorable lover and the cuddlesome son. He was so obviously frail.

Frail's a strange word to use for 300 pounds of oil-drenched Italian flesh, but frailty shone from him. He longed to, needed to, be loved. You could see it in that great letter-box smile, in the sense of self-conscious performance. He was pleased with himself, but yearning.

And he sweated. His theatrical masterstroke was not to pretend that he didn't sweat, but to make a point of it, patting at his forehead with a handkerchief the size of a beach towel. It was so human, so convincing.

But it was showbiz too. By all reports Pavarotti could be petulant, petty, sulky, demanding, acquisitive, vain. But when he opened his mouth, all that fell away like litter. The voice took over.

Perhaps there have been better voices. As I say, I know nothing. But, for whatever reason, his was the voice we heard and when we heard it we soared. You soared, I soared and most remarkably my electrician soared. My electrician's musical tastes had previously embraced only anodyne commercial pap. But when he heard Pavo bash out 'Nessun Dorma' at the World Cup, he went straight to a friend who knows about music and asked for a cassette tape for his car. Side one had to consist of Pavarotti singing 'Nessun Dorma' time after time. So did side two. The electrician's Toyota station wagon became La Scala on wheels.

Why? Why did my electrician fall for it? Why did you and I? Why did 50,000 people turn up at the fat man's funeral?

It was, I suggest, a combination of that endearing human frailty, and a single note. I don't know and don't care whether the note was one of the high Cs that Pavo was apparently known for. All I do know is that 'Nessun Dorma' swells towards that single note with the insistence of a building wave. It requires the singer to reach down into himself and up for the note and then to hold it as the orchestra beats and rolls behind him. And as the frail Italian fatso hit that note and held it, his uvula trilling, you and I and an electrician rose with him and for a moment transcended the mundane. The music lifted us beyond a muddied and imperfect world to a plane where we can't live but to which we can and do aspire. A plane of emotional intensity, of beauty, and of something resembling hope. Hope that things might be OK.

Do I go too far? If so, please explain why that one song, that one note, is burned into your mind and mine. Explain the adulation that surrounded old Pavo. And explain why we have heard nothing, not a squeak, from the puritans.

You know who I mean by the puritans. I mean the gym-going, butter-eschewing moralists of our age, the crusaders against fat. By rights they should have been ecstatic.

Three hundred pounds of chubbychops had just keeled over at the age of 71. Here was the chance for the advocates of scrawn to leap up and down like gibbons, pointing fingers, chattering their teeth and squealing, 'I told you so. If only he'd gone for the broccoli and tofu, he could have clung on till 75.'

Here was their chance. Why didn't they take it? A decent respect for the recently dead? Don't make me laugh. These people make a living out of ignoring the most fundamental rule of decency and respect, which is to let people be. No, decency doesn't come into it.

What does come into it, I suspect, is that the bullying fools, the guilt dispensers, the health zealots who disguise the delight they take in telling others what to do behind the pretence of caring, knew that the voice had it right and they had it wrong. Their creed is that the sole purpose of life is to stretch it out as long as possible. That note in 'Nessun Dorma' says something else. It says that what matters is not that you stretch life long but that you stretch it wide. The voice of old Pavo did what only art can do. It soared and reached towards a realm that the broccolists can't compete with, can't even imagine, something greater, older, wiser and grander.

I think the thin-minded puritans sensed this and it shut them up. So, good on you, Pavo. Rest your plump bones.

Yes

Yes is a corker of a word. Indeed I'm not sure that a better word exists. But do we use it? No, we don't. And neither did the Romans.

I know so because I asked J.B. Williams, our Latin master, aged 12. J.B. Williams wasn't aged 12 of course. Like all schoolmasters back then, his age was measured in geological time. But he had a pipe and malaria and he was stern and he was strong. And he knew the answer to my question. 'No, Bennett,' he boomed. 'There is no word in Latin for yes.'

The closest Latin could get to yes was 'ita vero' meaning 'thus truly'. The Romans were so strong and stern they had no need of yes.

Wouldn't that road look better with a bend in it?

No.

Will you stop invading our country?

No.

Do you realise that in a few hundred years your empire will be dead and your language with it?

No.

Do you further realise that you will become Italians with all the connotations that entails?

What are you doing with that sword?

Yes and no are the first words you learn in any foreign language. They're a cracking pair. No is the raised hand, the crossed legs, the fierce stare. It reeks of integrity. I have weighed up your proposition, it says, and concluded according to my own scale of moral reference that it is depraved, despicable and, above all, foreign. So no. With knobs on.

Most negatives in most European languages begin with n — nein, nicht, nyet, non, never, nunca, no. This could be coincidence, or it could be that they all derive from some remote proto-language. But I suspect it's because n sounds right. When you arrange your mouth to say no, your jaw juts, your neck stiffens, your eyebrows lower, your lips thrust like a carp's and your dental defences bristle. No is a roadblock. No is strong, independent and adult. No is authoritarian. No spitting, no smoking, no littering, no bloody arguments.

Yes, on the other hand, erupts from the throat as if greased. Yes opens the mouth. Saying yes makes you vulnerable, but it widens your eyes to the landscape of possibility. Yes is the yelp of the young. See all those y's. No coincidence there. Yo ho ho and yoicks. Yippee ay yay and yeehah. Let's yomp.

I've just invented yomp, but you can sense what it means. The meaning of a word is contained in the noise it makes. Yomp could only mean something clumsily cheerful, like fat women trampling butter.

(You won't believe this, but having written that last paragraph, I looked up yomp to check that I'd invented it. I hadn't. It means 'to march with heavy equipment over difficult terrain'. I knew you wouldn't believe me.)

Yes believes everything. But we rarely use the word. Instead we say 'yeah', or 'absolutely'. Of the two, 'yeah' is the more easily explained.

Pick the odd one out from this list: yes, oui, si, ja, da. It's yes, of course. The others all end in vowels. They leave the speaker open and yielding, with come-to-bed eyes. But the s on yes clamps the teeth down on the open and yielding, and issues a snake-like hiss.

Yes with an s is cautious. Yes with an s means 'yes but'. Bureaucrats turn yes into two syllables and they give the s the full treatment. The result means 'I am choosing to appear to agree with you but I've got more reservations than Arnhemland.'

When we really want to agree with something we say yeah. It isn't laziness. If it was, we'd also say lazineah. We say yeah because yeah sounds more yes-like than yes. But that doesn't explain 'absolutely'.

Absolutely is today's most common synonym for yes. Listen to the radio, the television, or a pub conversation and you will hear it constantly. I know I say it myself.

Absolutely is hyperbolic gush. It's like flinging your arms round another in a verbal hug, a hug that says, 'Oh crikey, I agree with you so very very much, and may I say what a pleasure it is to find myself in a non-conflict situation, because I am so contingent, vulnerable and insecure, so uncertain of my own identity and my opinions in this hostile world, that when given any opportunity to express agreement I behave like an affectionate octopus. Oh, please don't see me as threatening.'

Absolutely reminds me of Evelyn Waugh's *Scoop*. In it a newspaper magnate called Lord Copper is surrounded by underlings. Lord Copper is stupid but no one dares say so. If the underlings disagree with their boss, they say, 'Up to a point, Lord Copper.' On the rare occasions that they agree with him, they say, 'Definitely, Lord Copper.'

Does the popularity of absolutely mean that we are becoming like Lord Copper's underlings? Are we really just terrified sycophants? Have our spines crumbled that badly? And is that J.B. Williams over there, muttering 'Ita vero'?

Crossing the corporate ice ravine

'Oh,' she said, 'what a lovely puppy.'

'Yes,' I said, 'would you like to meet him?'

'I'd love to,' she said, 'but I can't right now. I'm crossing an ice ravine.'

'You're crossing an ice ravine?'

'Yes,' she said.

She wasn't crossing an ice ravine. She was balancing on a log in South Hagley Park. A man was balancing on the log with her. Behind them, other men and women were balancing on other logs. If any of them lost their balance, they would plummet several inches to a grassy death.

The technique they had adopted was to crowd together until one log was free of people. Then they nudged the free log forward and stepped onto it, just as one does on ice ravines.

Next door to the ice ravine another group of people were assembling something out of interlocking chunks of plastic. What the something was I couldn't tell because they had a long way to go. There was a pile of plastic bits still waiting to be fitted. My puppy pissed on the pile. The men in this group didn't notice. They were engrossed, as most men become when challenged to build something. The one woman in the group did notice. She was standing back and taking no part. She may have been standing back to reflect on the overall assembly strategy, but I don't think so because she threw me a coy smile and then giggled.

The smile was coy because there were yet more people present. These people had clipboards. As far as I could tell, they were not crossing ravines or building things, but assessing the people who were.

The edges of the ice ravine were marked by lengths of nylon rope. My puppy toyed with one. A clipboard holder noticed and said shoo. It was not the wise thing to do. I eventually retrieved the edge of the ravine by stepping on its trailing end as the pup ran past me. I returned it to the man with the clipboard but he did not say thank you. The pup and I went on our way. The pup was delighted by the sensory world and I was thrilled to have laid eyes on that legendary consumer of the corporate dollar, a team-building exercise. I felt I had witnessed the cutting edge of business.

The idea is wonderful. You take your employees out of the office into the threatening wilderness of Hagley Park, and you set them a task to perform. It is a task unlike any that they meet in their usual working day. And because it is so different and so challenging they become stimulated and their true characters emerge. You can then assess their leadership skills, their teamwork skills, their skill skills.

At the same time they learn about each other. By battling across the fearsome ravine they forge relation-ships with their workmates that they would never forge in the office. The result is honed and bonded employees who have been to Hagley Park and back with their workmates so that they are now bound in eternal friendship as if by hoops of steel. From that day forth the office hums with unity, with a willingness to die for each other and for the cause of corporate profit.

I was doing much the same thing with my puppy. As we galumphed around Hagley Park, I watched him carefully, noting his idiosyncrasies, his confidence with some things, his nervousness at a mower towed by a tractor. I played little games with him and rewarded him with bits of saveloy for doing what I wanted. By such means I will forge a bond with him that only death will break.

It isn't hard with a puppy. The puppy takes everything literally. The puppy is easily manipulated. The puppy has a brain that fulfils the needs of a dog but that has no notion of irony or absurdity. Nor, even more importantly, can the puppy put itself in my shoes and imagine what I might be thinking. It will never see the motive behind my actions. It's the perfect employee.

When the pup and I had finished our walk we came back past the ravine crossers. They had sat down to lunch. The food, laid on no doubt by the corporation, looked good to me and superb to the puppy.

The ice-crossing woman now had time to greet my pup. She knew what she was doing. She played a game with him and when he did as she bid she gave him a bit of free lunch.

'How's the team-building going?' I asked.

'Oh, I feel terribly bonded,' she said, and there was a tone in her voice and a light in her eye that dogs don't do. The pup and I went on our way.

Bloody Sunday

How do you waste your Sunday? I like to read about the Minister of Education's plans to revamp the NCEA. Then I go down to my study and waste some electricity. The electricity in question is the stuff in my head, the little charges that scuttle down the neural pathways, igniting ganglions as they scuttle, connecting ideas, turning them into words and turning those words into a column on the subject of the Minister of Education's plans to revamp the NCEA. And the effect of that column will be, as we say in the trade, zilch.

In what I laughably refer to as my career, I've written about 1000 columns and collectively or individually they have managed to affect the swing of the world not one jot. I know so. I have written, for example, with all the vigour of which I am capable, about diets, the zodiac and the myth of French sexiness. The effect? Good sensible English-speaking women still swoon when they come within 20 paces of an illiterate Parisian plumber merely because he rolls his r's. And when he spurns them because he's blind to the self-evident signs of infatuation — the roseate neck, the widened pupils, the coyly lowered chin, the fluttering finger tips — those same intelligent women head for the latest edition of *Slimming Weekly* to study the before and after photos — oh, the wonderful waistline of those slacks in the before photo, like the mouth of the Lyttelton road tunnel — and commit themselves to a month of chicken breast and broccoli. They then check the astrology page to see which day of the following month would be propitious for launching another assault on the redoubt of Monsieur Le Plunger.

So I know I'm wasting my time, my energy, my neurons and my life. No column I write will ever have any effect. At best, people may nod and say, yes, bang on, couldn't agree more, and then return to the garden to pot delphiniums or do naughty things in the potting shed under the guise of potting delphiniums. And then they'll have lunch. That's at best. At worst, they'll write me the sort of letter that corrodes the postbox. And then they'll have lunch.

I know so. I have evidence. A year or two back I wrote rudely about the Ministry of Education, partly because there is no other way to write about the Ministry of Education, but also because they had launched what they chose to call an initiative. It was to do with teaching 'values'. By now this initiative will have been in force for a couple of years and you will have noticed the extent to which values have improved among the young.

My point at the time was that values weren't learnt in school. And anyway schools don't and shouldn't exist to teach kiddies to be loyal and upstanding citizens who join Kiwisaver at the first opportunity, shop for food with ticks on it and wear sunscreen even on cloudy days.

The principal protagonist in the values column was the woman in charge of curriculum development, or some similarly worrying title, at the Min of Ed. I christened her Minscum. I wasn't nasty about her personally — for all I knew she might be a candidate for canonisation, a volunteer firefighter and patron of the local League for Dumb Chums — but I was as rude as possible about the educational theory for which she spoke.

No response from the Min of Ed. A few months later, however, at a gathering of educational people, a woman approached me, smiled with the warmth of Jesus and the charm of a child, and said, 'Hello. I'm Minscum.'

You can imagine my reaction. I curled both arms about my skull in the instinctive manner of a man in an air raid. At the same time I swivelled to evade the plunging stiletto that at that very moment would be seeking a gap between my short ribs en route to the soft essentials. But no bomb fell. No stiletto plunged. I opened my eyes. She was still smiling.

'I just wanted to thank you,' she said. 'We all thought your column was a hoot. And they still call me Minscum at work. Can I buy you a drink?'

See, it's futile. Stuff goes on going on, regardless of its absurdity and regardless of how much that absurdity is pointed out. And this is especially true of bureaucracies. You can't wound a bureaucracy. The blade just won't go in. One bit of the giant flabby mass may yield a little at the pressure, but another will expand in compensation. So I simply can't be bothered to explain yet again the wretched wrongness of the NCEA or how it is short-changing children and emasculating teachers, or how no amount of tinkering with nomenclature, or assessment modules, or methods of moderation or any other bits of the ghastly jargon that is associated with it, will make it right. So I'll just toddle down to the potting shed of happiness and find a juicier way to waste my Sunday.

Baz

I was going to write about, well, it doesn't matter what I was going to write about. My dog died. His name was Baz. He was six years old. For the first time in 20 or so years I woke on Wednesday as a man with no dog. I didn't know what to do. For 20 years I've got up and patted and talked to a dog or dogs. Then I've fired up the coffee machine, gone with the dog to fetch the paper, drunk the coffee, smoked a cigarette, gone to the toilet with the paper, then dressed and taken the dog out, or the dogs. Whatever the season, whatever the weather, we've gone to the hills or the beach for a scamper and it has felt right.

On Wednesday morning, I made coffee and fetched the paper and went to the toilet and then, well, nothing. Emptiness stood before me. It was like looking down the throat of a huge fish. I thought of going for a walk anyway, but I couldn't see the point. I don't walk for me. I walk for the dogs. It's my gift to them.

Now I have the gift of freedom. Freedom from buying dog food, from pulling on gumboots at seven in the morning, from having to make arrangements when I go away. But it's a gift I don't want. Freedom feels like imprisonment. In a vacuum of self.

A month ago Baz was a well dog. Or he seemed a well dog. He must already have had cancer, but he showed nothing. He was gleeful. He accepted all gifts. He gave none except his own wholeheartedness. Then symptoms showed. When the vet cut him open, he found the tumours that would kill Baz slowly. I said not to wake him and I drove to the surgery and I injected the lethal stuff myself. And I brought him home to bury him. On a hill, next to Jessie who died on Good Friday last year. I got blisters on my hands from digging his grave. They will heal. He will not.

Death isn't anything. You can't define it except in negatives. You can define a dog's life — its zest, its hunger, its lust. But not its death. It is just a cessation, a full bloody stop. Beyond which, nothing. It's a change of tense from is to was. Irreversible, and like nothing else, emphatic. In a smudgy world it's pure black. It absorbs everything, instantly. It's a line drawn under. It's an end, a terminus. It's not a debating point. It can't be bought off.

And it's tough to take. Too tough for many. Too tough for the dingbats of California who pay silly sums to have their dead flesh frozen in the hope of eventual resurrection. But the dingbats are easy to understand. Because of death's unique finality, and because we alone have the wit to realise that what has happened to another will happen to us, we've always sought a mental escape from death. And the free market has always been happy to supply that need. To exploit it. Hence cryogenics, the Pope, the Mormons at your door, the Islamic bombsters, mad Tom Cruise evangelising for Scientology, shamans, witch doctors, mullahs and the bristle-bearded, earnest archbishops whose voices make me squirm with rage. All of them deluded and deluding, all of them selling snake oil, all of them, every bloody one. Because death is tough. Because what seems unstoppable and good — the life of a dog, a rat, a lover — is finite. Because death happens.

Several people have told me that after their dog died they never got another one. The grief at the death outweighed the joy of the life. That grief is perfect. It's untinged by anything like relief. Dogs are whole of heart. People aren't. Dogs are simpler. Dogs appear to love us as we yearn to be loved. Dogs appear to trust us as we want to be trusted. It seems fairer for people to die, muddied, part-hearted people, than for dogs. Dogs tell no lies. Dogs conceal nothing. Dogs relish. Dogs harbour no grudges. Dogs don't prejudge us. Dogs don't watch rugby or porn or the evening news. Dogs have no money or clothes. Dogs don't go door to door selling insurance or handing out pamphlets.

I miss Baz. All sorts of reminders can make my eyes well. But I miss him less today than I did last Wednesday. And a month or two from now I'll be able to visit his grave unmoved by anything other than fond memory, by gratitude. And I'll have another dog by then. Similar size, probably, and identical joy. Identical zest, relish, bounce, honesty, life.

In his brief life Baz bit only one human being. It was a Jehovah's Witness.

Signs

Not being tall, black, devoted to civil rights or dead, I have little in common with Martin Luther King. But, like him, I have a dream. Indeed I have a lot of dreams.

I dream of a world in which any airline that thanks me for choosing it goes belly-up, and so does anyone who says 'Enjoy'. I dream of a world that pays no attention to Paris Hilton, burger ads, motor racing or *Dancing with the Stars*. I dream of a world where anyone talking of an obesity epidemic is strung up by their scrawnies, and where people in rich, safe countries acknowledge they are rich and safe, smile constantly at their good fortune and say thank you. I dream of turning on the telly at six o'clock to hear a recorded voice saying 'Nothing happened today that you need to know about. There will now be some nice music.'

I dream of a world where governments who ask for emergency powers don't get them. Because some governments with emergency powers abuse them by attaching electrodes to newspaper editors and the rest just screw up by shooting Brazilian electricians or arresting doctors because they look like terrorists.

I dream of a world in which the words 'drizzled', 'jus' and 'compote' are banned. And I dream of a world without signs.

We have too many signs. Most of them warn us about things. Warning: contents may be hot. Warning:

low-flying aircraft. Warning: falling rocks. Warning: shampoo should not be taken internally. Warning: keep out of reach of children. (This last one is actually wise advice, but it wasn't meant to be.)

They could all be replaced with one sign. That sign is the red triangle with an exclamation mark in it. It would be used to mean, 'Watch out for everything. You're still unlikely to survive till lunch because this is an endlessly hostile world and you are utterly incapable of looking after yourself, but don't come bleating to us when you catch a nasty, because WE WARNED YOU. By erecting this sign we are absolved of any legal responsibility when you are crushed, burned, mutilated, robbed, raped, ripped off, decapitated by a remarkably low-flying aircraft or maddened to the point of homicide by a few swigs of shampoo.'

I have just been overseas for three weeks. The country I went to should have had a sign at the airport. Warning: this country is hot, poor, violent and corrupt. I loved the place. And if there had been such a sign I would still have loved it. Because like most Westerners I have become inured to warnings.

My return journey required four separate flights. The nearer I got to home the longer the safety warnings became. On the last flight from Auckland the instructions about what to do in 'the unlikely event of an emergency' — and the use of the word 'unlikely' deserves a prize for patronising redundancy — and the descriptions of precisely what the authorities would enjoy doing to me if I locked myself in the toilet and lit a cigarette finished just as we landed at Christchurch.

Driving home from the airport I soon discovered that the sign people — they are answerable to whom exactly? — had not been idle in my absence. They hadn't pulled any signs down, of course. Signs are dismantled about as often as laws are. But at the entrance to the Lyttelton road tunnel, a new one had gone up. It was a big electronic one. I read it at a glance and I haven't stopped puzzling about it since. 'Transit supports safe driving', it said. Being something of a language buff, I know what all four of those words mean. But I don't know what the sign means.

Transit is the authority that maintains roads, including the little stretch of motorway leading to the tunnel. So in a literal sense I suppose it does support safe driving. But by the same token it supports boy racing, and cars driven by deaf, agoraphobic and astigmatic pensioners who can't see over the dashboard.

So I can only assume that the word supports is metaphorical. Transit supports safe driving in the same sense as other people support the All Blacks. In other words Transit favours safe driving. Transit doesn't want you to crash.

Well now, are we supposed to infer that other road authorities do want us to crash? Is Transit implying that the city council, for example, likes a bit of carnage on its tarmac? If not, why is Transit telling us this stuff? And who decided that it should?

The answer, I think, is that this sign belongs to the notorious family of Mission Statements, a family responsible for some of the world's ugliest and most dishonest children. And I have a dream. A dream that tomorrow I shall drive through the tunnel and find it gone.

Fat chance, perhaps, but if you don't have a dream, how you gonna have a dream come true?

This is the life

Three in the morning in a back street in Hong Kong and I've got a woman on each arm, tugging.

The one on my left arm is urging me towards a black curtain. Behind it lies her brothel. 'Come on, sir, come in. Beautiful girl. Come look see.' Her pitch is practised, smiling and slick. It has worked on a thousand beer-lit Westerners.

My other companion's a beggar. She's 30-ish, toothy, short. Her hair straggles and is knotted. As urgently as the madam is tugging on my left arm, she is tugging on the right. Her fingers dig into my flesh and she wheedles. 'I am really hungry,' she says, piteously, repeatedly, stretching the last syllable into a whine. I suspect these are her only words of English. She may not even know what they mean. She just knows that they have sometimes worked on beer-lit Westerners.

'I'm sorry,' I tell her, and turn to the madam.

'No thank you,' I tell her.

Each woman responds by grasping my arm a little tighter and winding the pitch up a notch, a wider smile to my left, more pain in the voice to my right. 'I am really hungreee . . . beautiful girl . . . just look see . . . hungreeeeeee.'

The women want money, my money, any money. This is business. Hong Kong is business.

All cities are, I suppose, but Hong Kong never pretends otherwise. Paris may pretend, London even, but Hong Kong is nakedly financial. It exists to trade. Crammed between sea and mountains, for a couple of centuries it has been one of the few places where East has met West commercially. For 99 years it was leased to Britain, though that makes the arrangement sound nicer than it was. The Brits got their imperial hands on Hong Kong through guns and greed. But the result was a prosperity unrivalled anywhere in China until that country's recent resurgence.

People flock to prosperity. They are doing so now in Shanghai and many of the east coast cities of China, but they've been doing it longer in Hong Kong. In consequence Hong Kong is the most densely populated spot on the planet. Hong Kong feels like the human equivalent of the shallow and caustic lake in Africa to which most of the world's flamingos migrate every year. The birds there form a single mass of feathered pink.

Or perhaps more aptly, Hong Kong reminds me of one of those rush-hour trains in Tokyo where stout women in gloves push the human cargo aboard so that the doors can close. As you arrive in this city you feel that someone will have to leave to make room for you. The most valuable commodity here is land. Every scrap of it is sold time and time again by vertical replication. On the way in from the super new airport, you pass forests of tower blocks, slim as pencils and 40 storeys tall. I have been inside a flat in one of those blocks. It was the size of my lounge. A family lived there.

An earthquake here like the one in Sichuan and, well, you just don't think about it. There's business to do. The business of becoming rich. The rich are envied as they are envied everywhere, but here they are also admired.

Openly admired. Wealth is celebrated. Money is good.

Every cranny of the city is given over to commerce. Every shop assistant is alert. Finger an item and you are instantly attended to, followed. They'll measure you for a suit and deliver it eight hours later. There's nothing, no good, no service, that you can't get here for money.

Food abounds: vegetable markets, meat markets and restaurants of all descriptions, many of them fronted by tanks of huge lugubrious fish. None of the food comes from here. The sea is too foul and land is too valuable. You can't farm on 40 storeys. And anyway you wouldn't want to eat anything grown here. The city sits beneath a permanent hazy hat of human-generated dirt.

And no one seems to care much. Night and day the place thrums. Naked self-interest shapes everything. There's little in the way of social security. You scrabble in the raw.

I came here to promote a book. A little event, held inevitably in a restaurant, drew no Chinese but a few curious Westerners. I met Danes, a South African, several fruity English people, a New Zealand woman with whom I used to walk dogs, and a former pupil who's now a lawyer for a cigarette company. They all liked being here. I do too. It feels like the inevitable consummation of human activity, unclouded by self-delusion.

After the bash, I went out into the night. It was like daytime minus 10 degrees. The streets were as busy. The enterprises open were different ones, but as numerous. The bars bulged with people and noise. And business grabbed me by both arms and felt for the wallet that makes me desirable.

The plank revisited

Remember the Abflex? It sold by the million.

Remember the Power Rider? It sold by the million.

Remember the Plankerciser? It sold none. Not a single unit.

Six years ago I invented and wrote half a column about the Plankerciser. At the time it seemed a certain winner. It was cheap and it had no baffling assembly instructions because no assembly was required. There was no need even to take it out of the box because it didn't come in a box. With the Plankerciser what you saw was what you got. To the inexpert eye it looked like a plank of wood stamped with the Plankerciser trade mark. For three easy payments of an arbitrary sum you received the Plankerciser by courier direct from the manufacturer, me, thereby cutting out the middle man.

The Plankerciser was designed to slide neatly under the bed and stay there. Once there it was so forgettable that you forgot about it and just went on with your life as though the notion of attaining the body of a Greek god with which to dazzle beachgoers had never crossed your mind.

I assumed that once I had invented the Plankerciser the world would beat a six-lane highway to my door, a highway groaning under the weight of grid-locked credit cards. It didn't. The path to my door is still a path. And it's knee deep in weeds. Now I know why. The answer is one word: marketing.

The truth came to me yesterday when I read a full-page

ad for Power Plate, 'the health and fitness phenomenon sweeping the world today'. If I'd read this ad six years ago I'd now be lounging in the perpetual summer of prosperity with a bottle of Mumm, rather than writhing in Lyttelton's winter, knocking out words for a pittance.

The Power Plate ad is a model of its genre. I know nothing about the machine itself — for all I know the pounds may fall off like autumn leaves if you so much as look at the thing — but the ad's a belter. It exploits the full range of the plugger's art, beginning with celebrity endorsements. This century believes in celebrity and there is no force stronger than belief. So 'Sting and The Police use it to keep in shape when they're on tour', Clint Eastwood 'swears by it' and Hilary Swank has this to say: 'I love that with the Power Plate I can get a full workout at home in next to no time.' And if Ms Swank says so, who are we to gainsay her, because, as the text goes on to trumpet, 'where celebrities go, ordinary folks are sure to follow'.

Celebrity extends to shops too. Harrods of London 'has devoted a large central retail sales area to Power Plate equipment, complete with plasma screen', and if the plasma screen doesn't convince you of the virtues of Power Plate, what will?

Well, faith in science will. Power Plate has snapped onto that faith like a pitbull onto a pug. 'Remember high school physics? The force applied to an object is equal to its mass times acceleration.'

Perfectly true, of course. But what matters is not the truth of the science. What matters is the reader's faith in scienciness. All the reader remembers of high school physics is that it was dreary so he ignored it. But now, when time and greed and indolence have hauled his shoulders to his waist and turned that waist into a rain-water butt, it is time to beg forgiveness and hope physics will come to his aid.

The ad also does a nice line in circular arguments: 'Commanding an impressive share of the rapidly growing world market for this kind of futuristic training equipment, Power Plate is unchallenged in its dominance of the industry'. In other words, this equipment succeeds because it's succeeding. And consider the use of 'futuristic'. What does it mean? Precisely.

So far so impressive, but it was actually an insignificant line towards the end of the ad that really set my mental wheels aspin: 'The streamlined designs of the my5 and my3 models,' it said, 'fit comfortably into any home.'

In other words I was on the right track six years ago. So now's the time to relaunch the Plankerciser. I've already written the blurb.

'As walked by Hollywood superstars in *Pirates of the Caribbean*, the Plankerciser is tomorrow's equipment under today's bed. Remember PhD physics and e = mc^2, where e stands for exercise not taken, m for money spent and c for the clutter of fitness machinery in your bedroom? Well, the Plankerciser draws on the genius of Einstein to permanently remove your guilt over being fat, your guilt over spending money on equipment you never use and the constant irritation of having the stuff cluttering up your home. You've already seen the name Plankerciser mentioned numerous times in this very advertisement. So join the millions who will order the

Plankerciser, slide it straight under your bed, forget all about it and solve your exercise neurosis for good. You know it makes sense.'

See you in Rich City, my friends.

Eating posh

If you go for a posh dinner in a trendy new restaurant in the bang centre of central London at someone else's expense, then it's churlish to complain about the meal. Well, I'm a churl.

The restaurant had no name. In keeping with a chic urban trend, it was known by its street address — 130 Pretension Avenue, or some such. It's a form of branding that pretends to disdain branding, a public announcement that the restaurant doesn't need publicity.

And neither did it seem to. The place was heaving with women in their 20s and men in suits. The men had removed their ties, partly as a concession to playtime, but mainly so that they could talk more loudly about money. Or rather bray about money. The restaurant sounded like a donkey farm.

The four of us got a corner table for two. The manner of the bearded and aproned waiter implied that we were lucky to get it, and, in one way, we probably were. In another, we weren't.

Faux rustic furniture, long-stemmed glassware, lighting too low to read the menu, a loud and visible kitchen and an overwhelming sense of this restaurant being absolutely the place to be, the closest you could get to Importance Central.

The chalkboard announced that foie gras was on special at the price of a small but serviceable Japanese import. My companions all ordered it, so I did too. Years ago I discovered that I didn't much care what I ate. Since then I've always just said 'I'll have what he's having' and looked forward to the surprise. My companions then all ordered steaks, so I did too.

The waiter gathered up the photocopied menus and turned to go.

'I'd like my steak well done,' I said.

The waiter turned like a schoolmaster who's just been struck on the back of the skull by a missile.

'Our steaks are served rare,' he said. And that, as far as he was concerned, was quite clearly discussion over.

Etiquette books are by and large mute on the subject of what to do in such circumstances. But it seemed to me at the time that correct form would be to overturn the faux rustic table, seize the waiter by the shirt front, prod him in the chest with an index finger, say 'You waiter, me customer' in a Johnny Weissmuller accent, plant a sloppy kiss on his beard and flounce from the restaurant singing, fortissimo and con molto brio, 'These boots are made for walking' and then dive into the nearest pub thanking God for having kept my dignity intact.

I did none of these things. I said, 'What?'

'Our steaks are all served rare,' he repeated, with a condescension that worked on my throat like a pound of butter swallowed whole.

'So I can't have mine well done?'

'No.'

Do I need to spell out the monstrousness of all this, how a food snobbery had become compulsory, how the perceived superiority of raw meat over cooked meat had shifted from a dubious convention to a diktat, and how, above all, the commercial provision of a service had been inverted, transferring the power from buyer to seller? No, I don't think I do.

But I was a guest. Meekly I ordered the other item on the specials blackboard, an Arbroath Smokey at £20. An Arbroath Smokey is a fancy kipper. Then I took calming refuge in my wine.

The entrée consisted of a slice of foie gras the size of a wine biscuit, two slices of bread and two prunes. The pâté was fine, but seven and a half of our eight prunes went back to the kitchen intact. Curiosity had put the other half prune into my mouth. It took, at a guess, about £10 worth of wine to eradicate all traces of it.

Now, imagine for a moment that you are a restaurateur. What would you serve to accompany an Arbroath Smokey? No idea? Nor have I. And nor clearly did this restaurateur, so he solved the problem by serving it with nothing. My £20 kipper dish consisted of a kipper. Full stop.

I pointed this out to the waiter by means of an exclamation disguised as a question. 'Is that it?' I said.

'Yes,' he said, and left us once more.

But I was a guest. I extracted a few hundred thousand bones from my kipper, scraped the remaining flesh from the skin and ate it, thoughtfully, at approximately £3 a forkful.

My companions had more fun sawing at their steaks, which had been created by walking a cow past one of those free-standing outdoor heaters you see in cafés, then butchering it. The steaks came with chips that absorbed the blood quite efficiently.

Eschewing coffee, we had another bottle of house red,

so named because it was priced like one, and that was dinner done. The bill was paid by an expense account, as, I would imagine, was every bill in the restaurant that evening.

When I got back to the flat where I was staying, a friend asked how my evening had been. 'Lovely,' I said, and went to the fridge. I found only a beer and a large packet of KP salted peanuts. I opened the beer and ate all the peanuts. They were splendid.

The Mendacity Medal

And so we come to the main award of the evening, the Mendacity Medal. This prestigious award is given every year to a word or phrase that consistently means the opposite of what it purports to mean. We seek a word or phrase that operates like an air-raid siren, warning the hearer that a rain of untruth is tumbling from the sky.

I am delighted to say that the field this year was a strong one. The judges have whittled it down to five finalists, the first of which is the word 'honestly'. 'Honestly' has been described as the adverb that no speaker or writer ever feels the need of unless he is being dishonest. It is the verbal equivalent of guilty body language, a signal that meaning and utterance have gone separate ways.

Our second finalist was submitted by a reader and is a newcomer to the competition. The word is 'darling', a supposedly affectionate term derived originally from the diminutive dearling. It can be used in either a private or a public fashion, but in neither, says its champion, does it ever reflect the speaker's true frame of mind. Among couples it is used most commonly when one or the other has something to hide. Or else it resembles a bad weather forecast, delivered in a calm and even tone but warning of a stormy row brewing out to sea. In neither case does it mean darling.

The public use of 'darling' is most common in the theatre and I can vouch personally for its dishonesty. 'Darling, you were wonderful' is just about the cruellest review you can receive, matched only in my experience by the printed review of a friend's novel. That review ran, in full, 'This book smelt good when I burned it.'

'Interesting' was a surprise entry this year and one that impressed the judges. 'Interesting' is never used with malicious intent. Rather it is the word most commonly employed by the middle classes to express boredom. An interesting play is one in which the audience spent the second half longing for the curtain. And over a glass of medium-price sauvignon blanc, the phrase 'Oh, how interesting' is the verbal equivalent of a yawn.

As always there was a slew of entries from the world of commerce, many of which the judges had seen before. 'Unrepeatable offer', which relies on the fallibility of the consumer's short-term memory, failed to make the finals this year, as did those old chestnuts 'new and improved' and 'hurry, limited stocks'.

But 'disappointed' did make the cut. Its use is widespread in financial institutions, and once again I can vouch for the truth of this untruth. Years ago I got a letter from my bank. We were not regular correspondents. I was a poor student. It was a rich bank. But it hadn't got rich by ignoring its debtors. 'Dear Mr Bennett,' the letter began, 'I was disappointed to note that your account. . . '

Even as a young man I remember noting the magisterial dishonesty of 'disappointed', and I am glad to hear that the word is still doing service.

But as you may already have guessed, these four entries, strong though they are, are the runners-up. As is traditional on these occasions I have kept the worst till last. The winner of the Mendacity Medal for 2008, and frankly it could win every year, is the simple, and at first glance innocuous, 'the people'. So blatant a fib is it that it has become easy to overlook.

The one certainty with 'the people' is that it never has anything to do with the people. A country known as The People's Republic of Whatever is unfailingly run by a dictator who was last legitimately elected in 1955 and who has a penchant for having the people smacked on the head. He and his cronies hold most of the people's wealth in numbered bank accounts in the Bahamas.

When the charming Mr Mugabe speaks of his devotion to the people of Zimbabwe, he is so far removed from a world where anything means anything, he probably doesn't even know he is lying. But the charming Mrs Clinton has less excuse. When she announces that 'the American people don't quit and they deserve a president who doesn't quit', she knows exactly what she is doing. First, she is flattering her audience with a meaningless generalisation, and then, by a staggeringly dishonest twist of rhetoric, she is inverting the truth. Her ruthless and entirely selfish lust for high office makes Macbeth seem like a dew-eyed innocent. Yet she contrives to present that vice as a virtue in the name of the people.

I have every faith that the American people will see straight through the devious little darling. Honestly.

Impure thoughts

Today's subject is bottled Steinlager.

Petty? Of course it's petty. Petty is just the English transliteration of 'petit'. Petty means trivial and trivial's just fine with me. Trivial comes directly from Latin. Trivia is the stuff that gets discussed at the point where three roads meet. It's gossip, of no great significance.

I like stuff of no great significance. And I am wary of anyone who doesn't. It's given to few to fish for big stuff. Or rather plenty of people fish for big stuff, but it's given to few to catch it, to haul up a grand notion, an overarching something, a gleaming mental whopper. A truth.

As soon as someone lands such a whopper everyone clusters around and wants a bit of it. The whopper loses its gleam. It dies and becomes dangerous, which is where the metaphor and I must go our separate ways because, apart from a nasty little bugger called the weaver fish, dead fish aren't dangerous.

Big stuff is never quite right. If it were we'd have sorted everything out by now and be bored. But people still like to cleave to big stuff, to have their mind run on railway tracks laid down by another. (Oh hello, new metaphor. I wonder how far this one will steam.) It is always easier to run on existing tracks than to lay down your own. But where does the Train of the Big Idea take you? Derivative City, at best. At worst the town of War. And once you're on the train, Mr Bush, there's no getting off. You've climbed aboard and you go where it goes.

(What a durable metaphor this is turning out to be. Though metaphors are dangerous to prose. Metaphors can stop being illustrative and become dictatorial. They can carry your meaning away to somewhere you hadn't thought you wanted to go. Exactly like the Train of the Big Idea.)

We are trivial beasts. Our senses are attuned to detail, calibrated to register the small, the insignificant, the smell of a second-hand pillow, the whirr of a quail's wings. And that is the stuff we do well to contemplate. It is what life consists of. It is the bedrock of experience. And it is the stuff in which any truth we arrive at must be rooted. Though one has to be impressed by the ability of truth to sink roots into bedrock.

Concerning yourself with trivia does not necessarily grant contentment. Indeed I am standing right now in Trivia Meadow while the Big Idea Trains go whooshing past, their passengers all comfortable with their skinny lattes and their smug belief that they know they're going, and I am pissed off about bottled beer.

I have got into the habit of drinking Steinlager. Habit is as much of a tyrant as runaway metaphors, but for once I don't mind. Habit makes things simple. I just walk into the pub, flick a cheerful eyebrow and the barmaid reaches for the Steinlager.

Steinlager doesn't taste any better or worse than other beers, but I don't drink beer for its taste. Six bottles of Steinlager make me satisfactorily garrulous and open to mirth. Twelve supply a hangover that belongs in the Old Testament.

But Steinlager sales must have dwindled because the

brewers have felt the need to refangle the stuff. They've invented a new version called 'Pure' with a transparent label implying its virginity. The name taps into the touristic come-on of 100% Pure New Zealand, which is about as convincing as the notion that Great Britain consists entirely of thatched cottages, hollyhocks and fat white cheerful women in aprons called Mrs Cleavage the butcher's wife.

The Steinlager people then paid an American actor to sell the new brew. His job was to suck up to Kiwis, to issue flattery as transparent as the label on the bottle. So he congratulates Kiwis on their intransigent bloodiness of mind, their independence, their courage to stand out from the international herd by saying no. While doing so he encourages them to drink the new beer. In other words, he encourages them to behave like sheep, to do as he says, to be the opposite of intransigent nay-sayers, to be brain-dead, nose-led dupes of advertising.

The other night I walked into the pub and flicked an eyebrow. I didn't get a bottled Steinlager. I got a bottled Pure. I flicked another eyebrow.

'It's the new stuff,' said the barmaid. 'Try it.'

I tried it. It tasted OK. 'So what's the difference?' I said.

'It costs more,' said the barmaid.

'In that case,' I said, 'I'll stick with the old stuff.'

'Haven't got any,' said the barmaid. 'No one wants it any more. They want the new stuff.'

Draw your own conclusions. I'm going to the pub to drink any beer I've never seen advertised.

Going Joe's side

Some car insurance companies offer lower premiums to women. Insurance companies aren't fools. They've looked at the stats and concluded that women drive more safely than men. So when I slid into the front seat of a small grey car in central Auckland last Friday, I was delighted to discover not only that my driver was a woman, but also that there were two more women in the back seat. This would be a very safe journey.

It was the evening rush-hour. As we pulled away from the kerb a discussion began on the route that we should take. Had I been familiar with central Auckland I would have taken control and said authoritative masculine things like 'Turn right here'. And if I had done so, a joy would have been lost.

We were heading for a publisher's party and all three women were publisher's editors. In other words they were used to receiving an unsolicited manuscript, swiftly assessing it to be manure of such richness that it could grow prize marrows, and yet communicating this judgement to the author in such a way that no feelings were hurt.

In consequence the car was courtesy on wheels. The conversation was steeped in the virtues of collaboration, tolerance, respect for the views of others, and an intense delight in language and the world around us. It was how life would be if men didn't constantly shout.

Because these women would shrink from the arc-light of publicity, I shall call them Ms Driver, Ms Backseat

One and Ms Backseat Two. The conversation ran more or less as follows:

Ms Driver: Does anyone know how to get there?

Ms Backseat One: Well, we could take the motorway, unless perhaps someone has a better idea.

Ms Backseat Two: I think the motorway's a good idea. Oh, look at that! Tonis Hair Salon. Sometimes I want to go out in the middle of the night and paint in all the missing apostrophes. Honestly, how much would it cost them to get it right? It's not as though it's hard.

Ms Backseat One: There ought to be a special apostrophe paint.

Ms Backseat Two: They could call it Pedants' Emulsion.

Ms Backseat One: Yes, Pedants' Emulsion. Very good. With a giant apostrophe on the can. Er, do you think perhaps we should get into the left-hand lane? If we're going via the motorway, that is.

Ms Driver: Left-hand lane? Is that Joe's side or my side?

Ms Backseat Two: Joe's side. Go Joe's side now.

Ms Driver: Sorry Joe, I'm hopeless on left and right. Shall I go Joe's side now?

Going Joe's side now was not a cracking idea. In preparation for changing lane we had slowed rather a lot. Traffic behind us was banking up nicely. Traffic to either side of us was whizzing past. I said nothing. I was concentrating on my right foot, which was pressing an accelerator it hadn't got.

We managed to go Joe's side only because a Mercedes braked. It had little choice.

Ms Driver: Aren't some road signs ridiculous? I mean, look at that one. 'Be Prepared to Stop.' What exactly is one supposed to do?

Ms Backseat Two: It's the same with 'Warning: low-flying aircraft'.

Ms Backseat One: What about 'Always Turn Left with Caution'? Don't you think it gains added significance in an election year?

Ms Driver: I was given this dreadful book the other day called *The Story of the Failed Conquest of Somewhere or Other*. What on Earth was the editor up to? Couldn't they see it was an oxymoron? I mean, if the conquest failed it wasn't a conquest.

Ms Backseat One: Do you think we should turn off down Gillies Ave? Talking of oxymorons, what about 'Grey Power'?

Ms Driver: Or 'The Honourable Winston Peters'?

Ms Backseat One: Oh, very good. Er, if we *are* going to take Gillies Ave it may be a good idea to get into the left lane soonish.

Ms Driver: Left?

Ms Backseat One: Yes, Joe's side again. Er, but perhaps not right now. There, go Joe's side now.

Ms Backseat Two: Oh, well done.

Ms Driver: You're very quiet, Joe.

She was right. I was quiet. I could sense that I was also a little pale.

Ms Backseat Two (gesturing at a building): Isn't that it?

Ms Driver: Isn't what what? Gosh, what a strange sentence.

Ms Backseat Two: Isn't that building the one we're looking for?

Ms Driver: What building? I can't see a thing in these glasses.

At which point everyone in this happiest and most co-operative of cars fell about laughing. And we arrived safely. And the insurance companies put another tick in their incontrovertible statistical record.

Security

I stand with arms outstretched, like Jesus on the cross. But unlike Jesus on the cross, I am scared that my jeans will fall down. The belt that usually holds them up is passing through an airport x-ray machine. As are my bag, jacket, wallet, pens, coins, keys, reading glasses, nicotine gum, cigarettes and lighter. Unless, that is, I am in the Philippines, where the lighter will have been confiscated.

An officer frisks me with hands like questing butterflies. Up my legs they flutter, then over my buttocks, my back, my chest and along my arms, but not, I notice, over my crotch. So there's the answer. When my anger at being pointlessly searched in airports finally reaches such incandescence that I feel compelled to act, I'll tape a bomblet behind my scrotum with the detonator clenched between my cheeks. It will kill no one except myself and I won't make a pretty corpse, but I will make damn sure I take out a particular notice. You know the one I mean. It's the only notice in human history to forbid, on pain of imprisonment, the making of jokes. I am not allowed to crack a joke about bombs.

Jokes are essential to mental well-being. But all authorities hate them because jokes pierce to the truth. Jokes see through bogus seriousness and say, 'Oh, come off it.' The instinct to make jokes is a natural reaction to overweening authority.

The authorities have an obvious response. Airport security, they will say, is no laughing matter. Do I want planes to be blown up?

Well, no, but jokes won't blow them up. I acknowledge that the jokes might get tedious for the security staff, but there are plenty of professions in which bad jokes from the public are an occupational risk, not the least of which is being a columnist. And anyway, my point is that the security staff shouldn't be there to find the jokes tedious. There is no need for airport screening. (At Heathrow they even make you remove your shoes. It's an olfactory horror show.)

Last week I caught a plane from Tauranga to Auckland. I was not screened. I could have boarded that plane in a fully primed explosive waistcoat and with a Kalashnikov down each trouser leg. The plane had about 40 passengers, including a member of parliament. Many a suicide bomber has gone to his grave for a far less impressive bag.

Again the authorities have an obvious response. They will say that a line had to be drawn somewhere and it got drawn at Tauranga. Besides, terrorists wouldn't bother with a little plane like that. They want to make a bigger splash.

Well now, we flew to a crowded terminal at Auckland where even the most obvious psychotic — sweaty, unshaven and muttering ecstatically about a gross of virgins to come — could join a check-in queue unchallenged. Though why he would bother to go all the way out to the airport to kill people is unclear. He had only to board a bus or train in the rush-hour to guarantee himself a massive cull of the innocent.

Terrorists have been with us in one form or another for centuries. They change their ideological plumage, but not their nature. And they have always been spoilt for choice of targets. Vivaldi concerts, Women's Institute conventions, bridge clubs, dog shows, all are open to any dingbat dressed in dynamite and all are splendidly newsworthy.

Terrorism has two purposes. One is to frighten the public and the other is to disrupt it. So the best response is to carry on as normal and ignore it. Intrusive, time-wasting, expensive airport security is a victory for the dingbats. And what's so special about planes? Last year someone blew up 50 people on a London Tube train. The Tube still has no security screening.

The only answer I can think of is that planes brought down the World Trade Center. So the whole infuriating business of frisking at airports is, at best, a sop to the cowed American consumer. At worst it's a way for various governments to keep terrorism at the front of the public mind and thus to justify unjustifiable foreign policy.

In the light of that observation, are you willing to take the tiny risk of boarding planes unscreened? Good, because so am I. If every x-ray machine were biffed into the sea, the only problem would arise in the Philippines.

Outside the smoking room in Manila airport sits a security guard. He has a fistful of lighters that he rents to smokers who have had theirs confiscated. The lighters he rents for a small consideration are the confiscated lighters. For a slightly larger consideration he'll even sell you your own lighter back. That enterprising man would need to be compensated for loss of livelihood. And with a generosity born of irritation, I am offering to foot that bill. So how about it?

Packing

I'm off.

What a fine sentence that is. Brief, emphatic, simple as a punch and just dripping with independent vitality. I'm about to take the cutlass to the mooring ropes and set sail on the high seas of chance. All habits and ruts forsaken, gone, erased. Freedom looms ahead like a fat, ripe mango. The juice of liberty will drip from my lips.

Though actually I'm just off to the UK to launch another book into the waters of indifference and to do some publicity whoring, but any journey is better than no journey. Even this trip holds the promise of a sniff of mango.

'Move fast, travel light, and don't look over your shoulder,' said someone whose name I can't remember, and since I've just failed to find the line in the *Dictionary of Quotations* I suppose it may have been me. If so, then I was right for once, and the most important of the three injunctions is to travel light. Take a passport, some nicotine gum for the flight, and something to read — though in extremis and foreign lavatories the passport will serve. And that's it. Let chance do the rest.

The vital thing is to lug as little stuff as possible. But oh, how hard that is. We are stuff magnets.

Write down your salary and multiply it by as many years as you've been earning it. The sum looks like a lottery win. But where is it now? Where did it go? For sure some of it went on food, and more of it went on drink and other essentials. But is the remainder squirrelled away in a savings account earning you a little and the bank a lot? Is it hell? It's gone, frittered, blown on the wind like a dandelion clock. It went on stuff, the stuff that competes for suitcase space whenever you go away.

Clothes especially. Look at the high street. Every second shop sells clothes. The shops exist because we want them to exist. The rag trade is as old and as durable as human wishing. None of us is immune. I own more shirts than I could wear in a month. They hang in my wardrobe like so many alternative selves. And they want to come on holiday with me.

They pile on the spare bed. Take me with you, they wail like clinging lovers, you're sure to need me. And it's tempting to relent, because you just never know. Imagination is fertile, fear pervasive. For even though every day at home carries just as much potential for triumph or catastrophe as any day away, it doesn't feel like that. Elsewhere is unfamiliar and our imagination creates surprises. The threat of surprises is unsettling. So we seek reassurance, and we lug stuff with us as totems against a spiky world.

Women, I'm afraid, are especially vulnerable. I'm not sure why. I'm only sure of offending by pointing it out. Is it because women are traditionally nesters? Whatever the reason, many women seem to believe the number of outfits required on a trip is reached by multiplying the days spent away by four. They seem also to suffer from the notion that nowhere in the world except home harbours a washing machine.

Many years ago I ran a school boarding house in Canada. One Easter the wealthy father of one of my charges rang. 'Tell Jimbo,' he said, 'to pack for every possible climate.'

I helped Jimbo cram his suitcase with fur hats and sunscreen, got him to sit on it while I did up the clips — he was a fat and idle child — and then I packed him off in a taxi to meet his father. Over the course of the next three weeks Jimbo went round the world. He went to Alaska, Austria, Australia and 20 other places that didn't alliterate.

At the start of the following term I asked Jimbo how his trip around the big wide world of infinite variety had been.

'OK,' he said.

'Where did you like best?' I said.

'Rome,' he said without hesitation.

'Why Rome?'

'It had the best video machines,' he said.

The point of the story is not that Jimbo was the most gormless child I ever had the misfortune to teach, though he was. Nor yet is it that travel is wasted on the young. Nor even that the world is what you make of it. It is simply that Jimbo remained Jimbo regardless of where in the world he went. Even on Mars Jimbo would have been gormless. And we all, in our different ways, are Jimbo. We take our selves with us, and that's more than enough luggage for anyone.

Keeping it real

Western Australia is the real Australia, and I am Jack the Ripper. No really, I am. Look, here's my disembowelling knife, still dripping. I could sell it for thousands on Trade Me, but I'm a sentimental fool. I intend to bequeath the thing to the museum that's been established in my honour on the south bank of the Thames. They'll be so pleased to display it. I'm hoping they'll find some way to keep the blood looking fresh on the blade. There's nothing like fresh blood to haul the trippers through the revolving doors with their ice creams and their T-shirts saying 'I'm with Stupid', to gawp delightedly at sexual violence by proxy. It's reality, see. The punters just love reality, and I'm for real, like Western Australia.

You've seen the ads. A vast white sandy beach and you're the only person there — except for a girl in a yellow bikini who pops up realistically whenever you feel like a bit of swimming. In the real Australia you can drive for miles along the deserted beach in your Landcruiser, crushing insignificant life forms by the million with every revolution of your chunky tyres. Meanwhile the unpolluted sea is chocka with more significant life forms, placid marine creatures that like nothing better than to swim alongside you and the girl in the yellow bikini. Though of course, at any time, you can dangle a line in the limpid waters, haul out one of those placid life forms, kill it, cook it and eat it.

Dismiss any thoughts of unreal Australia. Forget jolly old Bundaberg where the rum-soaked natives play a form of golf involving a five iron and a sack of cane toads. Forget dustbowl Australia, where the starveling cattle shrivel in the heat and the farmers hang themselves. Forget the Aboriginal settlements on benefit day where the roads are littered with drunks. Come west to the real Australia.

Not that Western Australia has a monopoly on reality. Here in little old NZ, we've got a company called Real Journeys. They'll sell you a real adventure, which you can read about in the brochure before it really happens — the visit to the magical glow-worm caves, the real cream tea with the real farmer in the real woolshed right next door to the real souvenir shop.

If you lack adventurousness but still crave the real, there's always reality television. Here you will see life as it really is — a dozen unacquainted people, chosen for the likelihood that they will hate each other, who are then secluded in a house or on an island with real cameras. During the filming of a recent show, the father of one of the participants died. This news from the unreal external world was rightly kept from the contestant, so that she could carry on being filmed being real. That film, of course, was then rendered even more real by editing, so that all the unreal dull bits went and only reality remained, the glorious reality of feeling, fighting and sex.

It's hard to remember now, but in the bad old days, real meant dull. 'Back to reality,' we'd say, after an interlude of self-delusion. In those days the real world stood in contrast to an ideal world, a world of imagined perfection that we alone of all the species on the planet were able to conjure into being in our heads. We had numerous names for the ideal world. We called it God or Plato's cave or heaven or bliss. The authorities were constantly reminding us that the ideal world would be our reward for good behaviour. Good behaviour meant paying taxes, suffering disease, eating little, owning less and dying young without questioning the right of the authorities to be authorities. It's a trick as old as human society.

Inevitably a few peasants always saw through this trick. Wanting a slice of real cake now rather than a lot of fantasy cake later, they revolted, and power was transferred to the people. Except that it wasn't. Power is never transferred to the people, because the definition of power is that it is exercised over the people. Power is only ever transferred to different people. And they play the same trick.

In Western capitalist society the authorities that govern our behaviour are no longer church and king. They are corporations. Corporations are playing the same game as church and king once played, but with an exciting new twist. They've invented a new idealised world whose purpose is exactly the same as the old idealised world, but they've changed its name. They've inverted the language. They've called it reality. It's breathtakingly audacious.

The purpose is the same as ever, to inspire belief. Belief keeps the mob in a state of bovine docility and the powerful in power. Feed the plebs fibs, then milk them for cash. The corporation is the new church. It's all really neat, everyone's happy, the world is made new, reality is banished, and I'm Jack the Ripper.

The bastard my lawyer

My lawyer has sold me. I feel that I ought to be entitled to some if not all of the money, but the person to ask about that sort of thing is my lawyer so I may just let it go. Not because I'm a nice man. But because he is.

John Mortimer said that the only qualities needed to practise the law were common sense and reasonably clean fingernails. My lawyer's got both, but that's not why he's my lawyer. I used to play rugby with him. You learn a lot about people from rugby.

The world divides into backs and forwards. Lawyers are generally backs, or, as we forwards think of them, skitteries. My lawyer was a second five, apparently inoffensive, clean-shaven, not particularly imposing, and mildly spoken. But it took only a couple of games to discover that when things got tough he slithered like an eel and bit like something with rabies. The ideal lawyer, I thought.

Of course admiration is a two-way street. From watching me play he would have noted my excellence at delivering verbal threats. I can imagine him thinking, there goes the ideal client, shouting.

So when, over canned beer in some damp clubroom a couple of decades ago, he offered to do the conveyancing work on my first house for free in exchange for getting me onto his books, it seemed to both of us to be a marriage made in heaven. I'd acquired a genial-looking attack dog. He'd acquired a loudmouth who fought like a neutered lab.

The marriage has worked. We've rarely met. Separation is the best guarantee of any relationship. Over 20 years he's bought and sold the houses I've lived in, a process that has put a reasonable sum of money into his pocket but kept an unreasonable sum out of the pocket of some illiterate real estate agent with a clean car, bad breath, a worse dress sense and a certificate saying she had attended a course in the legal requirements of property transfer that lasted a whole morning and that therefore qualified her to cram my letter-box with unsolicited fibs, witter about indoor-outdoor flow and drive a Beemer.

Apart from that, from time to time my lawyer has amended my will in accordance with the fluctuations of my love-life, and he has correctly spelt the names of each of my dogs. (Which is more than the council ever managed. In exchange for 13 years of licence fees, a sum that went entirely towards policing other people's unlicensed dogs, Jessie officially went to her grave under the name of Joss. She didn't care. I tried not to.)

A couple of times I've taken matters to my lawyer and suggested we do something drastic. He has advised each time that we wait a bit, and I've gone along with waiting in the hope that he would see sense in the end, and sure enough in the end I've seen sense. So, as I say, it has been a perfect marriage.

But now it's divorce. Lawyers are supposed to be a force for generational stability — Suewell, Suewell, Suewell and Sons, that sort of thing — but not any more. The old world has liquefied. My lawyer is having a mid-life crisis.

He's roughly the same age as I am, which is the age at

which you first peep over the crest of the hill and behold the valley floor an awfully long way down and dark as mystery. Then someone taps you on the shoulder and you turn round to see a bloke with a scythe, 'No hurry whatsoever, sir,' he says politely, 'but your toboggan awaits.'

At which point you have two options. One is to launch yourself down the precipitousness, gathering as you go a set of crusty opinions, a pair of warm slippers with cocoa, an ingrained curmudgeonliness and a pendulous belly. The other is to put up a fight.

Character doesn't change. What was true on a suburban rugby field 20 years ago is true today. The loud-mouth forward has simply said, 'Rightio, whatever you think, Mr Scytheman', and at this very moment is gathering downhill momentum that will take him all the way to Senility City and beyond. But the second five has refused to be brought down in mid-field. There's a game to be won here and the final whistle hasn't blown. The bugger's decided to emigrate. His children have grown up and gone away, he can see no reason to carry on doing the same thing as he's been doing for 30 years, and he and his wife, another skittery, I suspect, are going to start again, to be young, to have an adventure, to do the things they've always wanted to do. So my lawyer has sold his clients, self included, to some multi-barrelled outfit in town whom I haven't played rugby with, and is heading off towards the try-line of happiness. And I wish him well, the bastard.

Between seven and ten

Many years ago when I was teaching, a kid asked a question. Most of his classmates were snoozing at the back as usual, or doodling absent-mindedly on their neighbours, but this child wanted to know the difference between the seven deadly sins and the ten commandments. And frankly, I couldn't tell him.

Mine was not a religious upbringing. I wasn't christened, I wasn't hauled to church each week, and no Sunday school teacher got to fiddle with my morals. I turned out atheist.

(Meanwhile, incidentally, the nice girls next door, four of them, and all four bespectacled, got the works. They were christened, hauled and serially fiddled with. Three of them are now missionaries. All of which, if you think about it, and I just have, would appear to say quite a lot for the power of indoctrination and not very much for the power of the Big Cheese.)

Nevertheless over the years I've acquired a sketchy understanding of Christianity and I've got time for most of it except the belief bit. Belief is comforting but silly. On behaviour, however, Christianity is all good stuff. The nub of it, it seems to me, is that we should be humble and we should try as hard as we can to love our neighbours. Not easy, but good stuff is never easy. I, for example, would have to learn to love Winston Peters, and he would have to learn to do the opposite.

But there I go being spiteful again, which brings me back to sins and commandments. I am still unsure of the difference between them. The sins are obviously things you shouldn't do, but from my occasional glimpses of the commandments, they all seem to be things you shouldn't do as well. They begin with 'thou shalt not' and then go on about oxen.

But I have just been browsing *Brewer's Dictionary of Phrase and Fable*, which I highly recommend as a book for the lavatory, or rather a book for you when visiting the lavatory, and in between 'Seven cities warred for Homer being dead' and 'Seven Dials' I found the seven deadlies.

Crikey, what a list. Let's start with gluttony.

In 1973 the United States of America spent $3 billion on fast food. In 2003 they spent $113 billion. In consequence they are now the fattest people on the planet. But Americans are also the most Christian people on the planet. Right this moment several hundred aspirants are striving to become the next American president and every one of them professes some version of Christianity. A non-Christian has as much chance of reaching the Oval Office as a glutton has of avoiding hell. Is there an inconsistency there?

Americans are able to spend all that money on hamburgers because they are richer than anyone else. Now I'm all in favour of wanting to be rich, but Christianity isn't. Avarice is another 14.285 per cent of the sins that will toss your immortal soul into the devil's toaster. Am I the only one confused?

Most of the money that Christian America doesn't spend on hamburgers and military hardware is spent on transporting their neighbours, the Mexicans, back to

Mexico, which is a strange way of loving them. Mexico is a Christian country too, but across the Rio Grande the Mexicans can see the promised land. They are prepared to risk their lives to get there, and their souls if they make it. They want to join in being fat, rich and damned. Does anyone take the seven deadlies seriously?

And then there's good old lust. If lust is deadly, then I'm dead, as is every ogler, fantasist, one-night-stander and self-abuser, every woman who's studied Dan Carter's underwear, and every visitor to any of the trillion porn sites that comprise at least half of the internet and that are nearly all hosted in, whoa, the most Christian country on the planet.

I would appear to be singling out the States and so I am, because the States is the world's boss. All nations either implicitly or explicitly aspire to the success that the States has achieved. We envy Americans their ease and prosperity. And, wouldn't you just know it, envy is a deadly sin too.

Both commerce and country urge us to want, lust, envy and consume. Indeed they require us to lust, want, envy and consume. The prosperity we cherish depends on us wanting, lusting, envying and consuming. If we didn't, if we became abstemious, unenvious and loving, the great engine of Western capitalism would stutter, stall and collapse in on itself. In other words, the long-running success of the ostensibly Christian West is founded as firmly and squarely on the seven deadly sins as my house is on the Port Hills. Which is all, frankly, baffling.

As was the kid's question that I began with. But I didn't admit to being baffled. I told him that the difference between the seven deadly sins and the ten commandments was simple. The answer was three. Glib, I admit, but on reflection I think that answer makes as much sense as anything else.

Warty

I didn't like him. He was warty, American and fat, but these things do not explain my dislike. I just didn't like him.

Warty was slumped on a bar stool in Shanghai. I suspected that if he stood up, the stool might remain plugged into his backside by suction. He was drinking a cocktail that resembled arterial blood.

He made some introductory remark, then launched into an encomium of the Western way of doing things, by which he meant the American way of doing things. It was a hymn to the West. We'd got it right. They'd got it wrong. USA 1, China 0.

China is a totalitarian state, he said. He was right. China has always been a totalitarian state. For several thousand years it had autocratic emperors. The current ruling communist party, which is about as communist as my dog, is merely another imperial dynasty, another chapter in the long story of this land. Like the dynasties it is unelected.

What Warty didn't say is that it is possible for an unelected authority to be benign. It is possible for an autocracy to do good. It is also possible to have a public examination system that brings the best people into government. The Chinese have had such a system more or less continuously for two millennia. You could argue that this makes for a better system than democracy does. I don't argue that, and Warty obviously wasn't going to, but it is possible to argue that.

There's no freedom in China, said Warty. There was truth in his words. Liberties that we take for granted are denied here. The Chinese press is muzzled. Few newspapers dare to snarl. There is effectively no political dissidence. In some parts of the country women are still forcibly sterilised. Prisoners are tortured. Labour camps exist. Homosexuality is no longer an imprisonable offence but beyond the major cities gays cannot be themselves. There is abundant corruption here among officialdom. All this is true. In the 30 years since murderous Mao, freedoms have grown and they continue to grow, but these things remain true.

Then Warty made me bristle like a brush. The people are brainwashed, he said.

Oh Warty, do you imagine that you are not? Do you imagine that your magnificent brain, so smugly articulate, does not run along railway lines laid down by the society that raised you? Do you believe, for example, that you have discovered for yourself the sentiments that you are now parroting to me? Do you think you're thinking fresh? Do you imagine that we in the rich West are not the victims of brainwashing all the way unto misery?

Come with me, Warty, and read the Sunday magazines. Look at the bombardment of lies we undergo, the commercial lies that urge us to feel a void of dissatisfaction, and to fill that void with food and cars and cosmetics and travel and tat and credit cards and Swiss-made watches and exercise machines in search of the better flavour, the greater experience, the tauter flesh, the happiness. Lies that come at us from all sides at all times, Warty, from screens and walls and radios and print. Look at it, Warty, and tell me it hasn't seeped into your clever skull and distorted your vision of the world, your proud freedom. And tell me, Warty, has it made us happy?

Walk the high street of any Western town and tell me what you see. Look at the faces, Warty. Then walk the streets of China. Watch and hear the ferocious rows that erupt in the streets like sand-devils and dissipate as quickly and end in smiles. Look at the vigour, Warty, and tell me who lives better, who lives happier.

Or watch the traffic here, Warty. See them driving motorbikes with children between their knees, children they cherish every bit as much as you cherish yours. See them accepting responsibility, not hounded by rules requiring them to fence their swimming pools or register their dogs or live in fear of accidents. Sure, they have accidents but they cope with accidents uncounselled because they acknowledge that there is a force in this world called luck and that we are all subject to it and that you cannot legislate it from the world.

Or visit a Western restaurant, Warty, and watch the couples sitting in candle-lit isolation, stupefied by boredom, but behaving according to the template of happiness as advertised. Then enter any restaurant here and watch the people being loud, people of all ages. Men, women, children, surrounding communal plates of food, not isolated in grim couples or stuck at home with a giant refrigerator and internet porn and a TV dinner, but belching and laughing and shouting and breaking off mid-meal to smoke, and no one cares. They are companions, which means literally bread friends. Can you truly tell me, Warty, that they are brainwashed and you and I are not? And explain why people live longer here.

All of which I didn't say. I left Warty plugged on his stool with his glass of blood and went out into the noisy Chinese night.

Safety officers

I'm in love, oooh, I'm a believer, I couldn't leave her if I tried.

Her, in the above quotation from those mop-haired philosophers The Monkees, is Dunedin. And I have, as it happens, left her. I have returned to Lyttelton, but only because that is where I am used to living and habit is a tyrant. Were I wise I would sell my house today for whatever price I could get and head south, south to Dunedin. When the word gets round, thousands of people will be doing just that. Because Dunedin's got, oh wonder of wonders, City Safety Officers. I've seen them with those popular proprietary ocular devices, my own eyes.

There were two of them patrolling George Street in hi-viz jackets. The moment I saw those jackets I realised how dangerous my own muted clothing was, how vulnerable it rendered me to the perils that lurk in every crevice of my life, how barely visible I was to the random homicidal motorist or the careering skateboarder. Since coming home I have bought a hi-viz jacket, of course, and some hi-viz pyjamas for nocturnal safety because you just never know.

But my hi-viz stuff is not their hi-viz stuff. Theirs was embroidered on the breast with the legend Dunedin City Safety Officer. When I read those words I felt as though I had sunk into a warm endorphin bath of security, an amniotic wallow. It was like being back at primary school when fleshy Mrs Coghlin and even fleshier Mrs Lamprey patrolled the playground, oozing maternal comfort to us tots and ensuring that none of us climbed too high on the climbing frame or ran too vigorously across the murderous asphalt yard.

I felt an urge to run to the officers and to embrace them. As their arms encircled me, I would weep with relief. Then, drying my eyes and smearing the snot from my nose with a sleeve, I would look up into their loving faces and murmur, 'Thank you. Thank you from the depths of my insecurity.'

But I held back. Why? Cowardice? Not a bit of it. No one could be afraid of their benign and swaddling presence, their almost luminous avuncularity. No, I checked myself out of consideration for the work that the officers did, and that my blubbering gratitude might prevent them from doing.

For any moment that I spent wrapped in their arms, though a joy to me, might prove a preventable disaster to others. While I unburdened myself to them, at that very moment in some DIY store elsewhere in Dunedin City, an innocent citizen might be buying a stepladder from a sales clerk too young or too criminally casual to do his duty. In consequence the purchaser might not be warned of the dangers of the top three steps of that ladder. And if, in his haste to remove an obstruction from his spouting — oh how sweetly the rain falls in Dunedin, like an aerial blessing, a kindness to the skin — he neglected to read the warning stickers on those top three steps he might, even as I was embracing the safety officer and crooning, tumble to the paving that surrounds his little bungalow and smash his skull and Dunedin's safety record to pieces.

Or because of my self-indulgence a swimming pool might go unfenced and a momentarily unsupervised toddler might meet a watery grave. Or at some unconsidered fast-food drive-thru a customer might power away from the little window clutching a coffee between his thighs and fail to read the warning on the lid, the one that says the contents may be hot. And if by some cruel chance he were forced to brake sharply by the passage of an ambulance hurtling to the house of the stricken man whose spouting was still blocked, he might, in the act of depressing the brake pedal, clench his thighs, pop the lid from his coffee and flood his lap with consequences too horrible to describe or contemplate. And all because of my selfishness, my love.

While I performed my act of grateful reverence, fatty foods might be bought willy-nilly. Some innocent might conceivably purchase a whole pound of bacon, streaky bacon at that, murderous streaky bacon, lug it home as the Greeks lugged the Trojan Horse to within their city walls, fry it, slap it between slices of white bread and — oh, share my shudders, readers — butter, and eat it.

So I let them be, the safety officers. I let them continue on their mission to render Dunedin City safe. As they passed me by, I just stared at them, as Wellington stared at David Beckham, with the mute and moonlike eyes of love. I'm a believer.

Drink with doc

Want to be happy? Drink with a GP. But avoid surgeons. Surgeons are just clever plumbers. Surgeons see pumps. GPs see hearts. The difference between a surgeon and a GP is the difference between porn and love.

GPs aren't allowed to tell you the stuff they've seen, of course, but I've found that beer works on most GPs like a knife on an oyster. And if beer proves blunt, there's always Scotch.

I drank with a doctor once who had been my own doctor for a while and then emigrated. I have no reason to believe that these facts are related. He emigrated with wife and kids to a Pacific Island. The family's arrival boosted the island's population by more than 1 per cent.

The day they arrived, a child on the island died. Doc went to the funeral. As the locals filed past the open coffin, they all threw something into it. Most threw money. Doc had no money with him. He was acutely aware of being watched. He threw in his signet ring.

The following Sunday he went to church because that's what you did on this island on Sunday. The pastor, or vicar, or Mormon elder, or thrice reverend Archimandrite, or whatever was the title of the old booby who ran the church and therefore effectively the island, greeted Doc effusively, as one does when greeting one's only avenue to the New Zealand medical system, and introduced him to his substantial wife. She proffered her hand. On one of her chubby fingers was the signet ring.

The doc said nothing. But a couple of years later, when he returned to New Zealand, he told me the story and I liked it so much that I bought him beer. So the ring wasn't a complete loss.

I drank with a different doc last month. If he's reading this he's probably trembling over what I'm about to reveal. He can stop trembling. For one thing he was disappointingly discreet. For another thing I couldn't get much beer down him. I suspect the two facts are related. He drank little because he was driving. Conventional morality condemns the misery caused by drunken drivers, and fair enough. But has no one except me noticed the disappointment caused by sober ones? In vino veritas. Sans vino chitchat. (And that, by the way, is the first trilingual three-word sentence ever published.)

But actually the evening was far from chitchatty. We'd not met before. My opening line was 'Let's have an evening without chitchat.'

'Good,' he said.

Life was never long enough for chitchat. And at 50, I just can't be bothered. I want conversation that exposes the pink and quivering meat a surgeon carves through without noticing.

'So tell me, Doc,' I said, 'what does it mean to live well?'

'Do you mean,' he said, 'what makes people happy?'

Ah, happy. We all want to be happy. Ask teenagers what their dreams are and some will say they want a Ferrari. They don't know yet that a Toyota is as good. Some will say they want true love. They've seen too many bad films. But nearly all will say they want to be happy. Ask them want happy means, however, and they'll struggle.

There's irony in the word happy. Hap means luck. To happen is to occur by chance. A mishap is a misfortune. Happenstance means the random blows of fate. So happy means merely lucky, blessed by fortune. It's unplannable, beyond our control.

'Okay,' I said, 'tell me what makes people happy. Has it anything to do with health?'

'Not much,' said the doc. 'Plenty of healthy people are miserable all the way unto the car exhaust.' (Though he didn't quite put it like that. Unlike me he isn't seduced by linguistic pomposity. He keeps things simple. He sees people who are sick. Sickness is a time for plain words. Fancy words are a mere Ferrari.)

'What makes people happy,' he said, 'is. . .'

'Yes?' I said.

'Hope,' he said.

'Hope?'

'Hope.'

Surely not, I thought. Hope's an illusion, doomed eventually and inevitably to be smashed on the savage reefs of reality or mortality or both. Hope's an old deceiver. The dangling carrot. The just-beyond-reach. Hope is tomorrow, next week, next year.

Achieve what you hope for and it's no longer hoped for. By its very definition, hope is forever unrealised. All of which I said, more or less, to the doc.

'Whatever,' said Doc. 'But there it is. I see unwell people every day. And the difference between the happy unwell and the unhappy unwell is hope.'

'So what exactly is it,' I asked, 'this hope?'

'It's having something to look forward to,' said the doc with enviable simplicity.

Is he right? I think he may be. Happiness is having something to look forward to. If you ain't got it, get it. I have. I'm looking forward to the next time I drink with a doc.

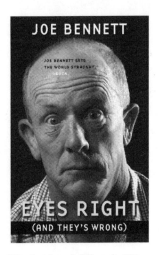

Eyes Right (and They's Wrong)
Joe Bennett

In the last year New Zealand's favourite columnist has turned fifty, lost a dog, been to China, been motivationally spoken to, built a goatshed, drunk with a Bangkok Buddhist, survived Christmas, eavesdropped Winnie with Condoleezza and . . . but why not let him tell you about it himself? *Eyes Right (and They's Wrong)* is Joe Bennett at his ruthless, funniest best. There's no more to say, really.

He continues to live in Lyttelton. Just.

HarperCollins*Publishers*

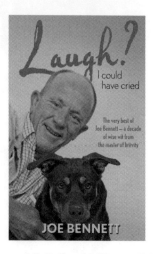

Laugh? I Could Have Cried
Joe Bennett

Joe Bennett was born into the middle classes of England in 1957. Life was stable, suburban and sunny. Computers weren't around to ruin his childhood, nor terror of paedophiles, nor fast food. He had it easy.

Aged 29, he came to New Zealand for one year to teach. Aged 51, he's still here. But in 1998 he swapped the classroom for the opinion page of the nation's newspapers. Since then, Joe Bennett has been Qantas Media Awards Columnist of the Year three times, he's had eleven collections of his columns published in New Zealand and three worldwide, he's written three best-selling travel books, he's become a regular on radio and television, and he has made far too many after-dinner speeches.

Laugh? I Could Have Cried presents the very best of a decade's work, organized by topic. Here are his most memorable thoughts on dogs, games, language, travel, the idiocy of belief, and the swamping trivia that shape our lives despite our best intentions, all of them written with the ferocious comic clarity that has made his name.

HarperCollins*Publishers*